# THE UNOFFICIAL

# GAME OF THRONES

## COOKBOOK

The Greatest Culinary Adventure Of All Time.
Winter Is Coming...So Eat, Drink & Make Merry.

# GAME OF
# THE UNOFFICIAL THRONES COOKBOOK
The Greatest Culinary Adventure Of All Time. Winter Is Coming...So Eat, Drink & Make Merry

ISBN: 978-1-912511-83-9

## Disclaimer

This book is unofficial and unauthorised. It is not authorised, approved, licensed or endorsed by George R.R. Martin, his publishers or Home Box Office Inc.

Except for use in any review, the reproduction or utilisation of this work in whole or in part in any form by any electronic, mechanical or other means, now known or hereafter invented, including xerography, photocopying and recording, or in any information storage or retrieval system, is forbidden without the permission of the publisher.

This book is sold subject to the condition that it shall not, by way of trade or otherwise, be lent, resold, hired out or otherwise circulated without the prior consent of the publisher in any form of binding or cover other than that in which it is published and without a similar condition including this condition being imposed on the subsequent purchaser. The content of this book is available under other titles with other publishers.

Some recipes may contain nuts or traces of nuts. Those suffering from any allergies associated with nuts or any other foods should avoid any recipes containing nuts, nut based oils or those ingredients to which they have an allergy or intollerance.

This information is provided and sold with the knowledge that the publisher and author do not offer any legal or other professional advice.

In the case of a need for any such expertise consult with the appropriate professional.

This book does not contain all information available on the subject, and other sources of recipes are available.

Every effort has been made to make this book as accurate as possible. However, there may be typographical and or content errors. Therefore, this book should serve only as a general guide and not as the ultimate source of subject information.

This book contains information that might be dated and is intended only to educate and entertain.

The author and publisher shall have no liability or responsibility to any person or entity regarding any loss or damage incurred, or alleged to have incurred, directly or indirectly, by the information contained in this book.

# Contents

**W**esteros, Essos and the rest of the Known World is such a vast land that exotic and exciting food can be found all over the realm. From the sumptuous feasts of King's Landing to the scavenged meals of the streets of Fleabottom, the foraged or pillaged dishes from the land beyond The Wall to the abundant decadence of the Free Cities - the world of Game of Thrones has it all.

Just like the unfolding plot, beware - all may not be as it seems with these recipes - magic, misdirection, tricks and manipulation may all be found within this book's pages. But unlike the fate of Joffrey and Myrcella Baratheon there's no poison to be found inside (although you may wish to go easy on some of the cocktails!). All of the recipes to be found within are delights fit for the King or Queen's table.

Taste your way around the Seven Kingdoms from the tropics of Dorne to the far North, feel dragon's breath and the icy chill of a White Walker on your cheek. Savour the sights and sounds of the lands as you embark on this culinary adventure. Treat your guests to feasts that wouldn't have looked out of place at the Red Wedding (although we don't recommend massacring them afterwards) or perhaps even the Last Banquet when we finally find out who will sit upon the Iron Throne for good.

For as sure as it is that an episode will bring death, drinking, nudity and dragons - so too will this book bring pleasures that even Little Finger's women couldn't compete with.

## Conquest Canapes

**N**o party fit for royalty would be complete without a bustling array of captivating canapes. Treat your guests like the Starks greet the Baratheon's in the first ever episode (but let's hope they repay you much better…). Have plates and platters piled high with Night King spears, dragon eggs and Hot Pie's hot pies. You'll be the talk of the Seven Kingdoms.

## Stark Family Starters

**A** feast must begin with a taste of what's to come, so what better way than by serving your guests a hint of exotic lands, from the blood oranges of Dorne to the seafood of Braavos these starters begin as they mean to go on with punchy flavours that will hit you harder than The Mountain hit The Red Viper, and like Daenerys after her boat encounter with Jon Snow- your guests will be left crying out for more.

# MAINS FIT FOR THE MOUNTAIN

It's not all feasts and fun in Game of Thrones land, times are hard and food often scarce; especially now winter is coming. So it's time to fill up with some hearty meals guaranteed to give you the strength you need to face the coming wars (or even a strange encounter with Ed Sheeran in the woods). These dishes are so tasty that anyone will be willing to bend the knee if it means you might cook for them again.

# DRAGON DESSERTS

There's more than blood and battles & doom and gloom in the world of George R. R Martin's imagination. There are cakes and fruits and beautiful spices. Admittedly you may not be alive for long enough to sample very many, so enjoy it while you can and get stuck in further than Jaime's sword in the Mad King's back.

# KINGSLAYER COCKTAILS

No one in the Game of Throne's universe seems immune to the lure of alcohol, with the exception of the fun-sucking Sparrows. Some like Tyrion even revel in being notorious for their ability to sink drink with the best of them. Most often red wine appears to be flavour of the day, drunk in copious amounts whilst glaring menacingly over the brim of an ornate goblet….but why be so samey?! Let's branch out a little and enjoy mixed delights from across the lands. Maybe even a Game of Thrones drinking game could be in order…

# WINTER IS COMING…

So cozy up my good friends. Eat, drink, be merry and raise a glass to George R. R. Martin.

For all the bravado, opulence and scavenging that plays a part in the gastronomic world of Game of Thrones, you'll be glad to know that all our recipes have a footing firmly in the 21st century. You can source all the everyday ingredients in your local supermarket and won't have to travel to far-off lands to find those precious spices.

We hope you enjoy playing a part in the greatest (culinary) adventure of all time.

# CONQUEST CANAPES

# Reek's Severed Sausage

## Serves 12

## INGREDIENTS

- 75g/3oz plain flour
- 1 large egg
- 125ml/4floz semi-skimmed milk
- 40g/1½oz beef dripping, lard or 2tbsp flavourless oil
- 12 cocktail sausages

## METHOD

- Preheat the oven to 220°C, 425°F, Gas 7.

- Add the dripping (or lard/oil) to a 12 cup steel muffin tin, divided equally between the moulds, and place it in the oven to heat for 10 minutes.

- Place a sausage in each indent and cook for 10 minutes.

- While this is cooking make the Yorkshire pudding batter by sifting the flour into a bowl and seasoning, then make a well in the centre.

- Break the egg into the mixture and beat with an electric hand or balloon whisk gradually incorporating the flour and milk.

- Remove the sausage tin from the oven and pour the batter into the sizzling hot fat. Be very careful as the oil is very hot.

- Immediately return the tin to the highest shelf in the oven.

- Cook for 20-25 minutes or until the puddings have risen and become crisp and golden.

- Serve as soon as possible: They're delicious on their own but horseradish, mustard or cranberry dips would all make wonderful additions.

## ◄ CHEF'S NOTE ►

*Poor Theon Greyjoy may be less intact than at the beginning of the series but his loss is our gain, these tasty severed sausages are the perfect way to begin a feast fit for King's Landing.*

# Dothraki Blood Pies

## Serves 6

## INGREDIENTS

**For the pastry**
- 300g/11oz plain flour
- ½ tsp salt
- 175ml/6floz warm water

**For the filling**
- 2 cloves garlic
- 1 small onion
- 225g/8oz lamb mince
- 225g/8oz black pudding/blood sausage
- Vegetable oil

## METHOD

- Make the pastry by mixing the salt and flour and keep adding water in small quantities to make a dough.

- Divide into two halves. Roll each of the halves into a rope of equal sizes. Cut each rope into 3 pieces.

- Dust your surface with flour and roll out each piece of pastry into a circle.

- Mix all of the filling ingredients together and add filling to each of the discs, leaving ½ inch border untouched at the sides. Join the edges and crimp them together with a fork.

- Once all the pies are ready, heat the oil in a deep fat fryer or a deep pot until a small piece of bread browns but doesn't burn when added to it.

- Fry the pies for 5 mins or until golden.

- Put the cooked pies on paper towel so that it soaks up the excess oil and then serve.

## ◀ CHEF'S NOTE ▶

*On Daenerys and Khal Drogo's wedding night 'food was brought to her, steaming joints of meat, thick black sausages and Dothraki blood pies.'*

# Dragon Eggs

## Serves 12

## INGREDIENTS

- 6 eggs
- 1 tbsp mayonnaise
- ½ tsp salt
- ½ tsp pepper
- 1 tsp mustard
- 1 tbsp paprika powder to garnish

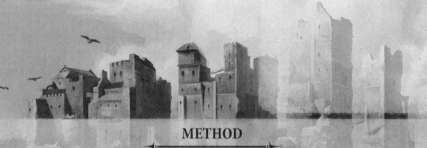

## METHOD

- Boil the eggs by placing in cold water, bring the water to a boil and cook for 10mins.

- Place the eggs in cold water and leave to cool for 5mins.

- Peel the eggs and slice in half lengthwise.

- Scoop the yolks out and place in a separate bowl.

- Place the eggs whites on extra plate.

- Add all the other ingredients (except paprika powder) to the yolks and mix until creamy.

- Divide the mixture between the yolk holes on the egg whites, then sprinkle with the paprika powder to serve.

### ◄ CHEF'S NOTE ►

*It's hard to remember but way back at the beginning of the series Daenerys was a nobody, pimped out to Khal Drogo in order to help her brother reach the Iron Throne. That all changed when she was gifted three dragon's eggs as a wedding present.*

# 'Horse' Jerky

## Serves 8

## INGREDIENTS

- 450g/1lb boneless top round or sirloin steak
- 60ml/2floz liquid smoke
- 60ml/2floz soy sauce
- 60ml/2floz Worcestershire sauce
- 1½ tsp kosher salt
- 1 tsp black pepper (freshly ground)
- ½ tsp garlic powder
- ½ tsp onion powder
- ½ tsp cayenne pepper (or to taste)

## METHOD

- Wrap the beef in cling film and freeze for 30 to 60 minutes until firm, but not frozen solid (this will make it easier to slice evenly later).

- Using a sharp knife, slice the beef across the grain into thin strips about ¼inch thick.

- Place the liquid smoke, soy sauce, Worcestershire sauce, salt, pepper, garlic powder, onion powder, and cayenne pepper in a large zip-top freezer bag; seal and squish to combine.

- Place the beef strips in the marinade, re-seal, and toss to coat. Open bag, squeeze out all the air, seal, and refrigerate for 12 hours or overnight.

- Preheat the oven to 130C/250F/Gas ½.

- Drain the meat strips from the marinade and pat dry with paper towels.

- Arrange the beef strips on a baking rack in a single layer with room in between.

- Bake for about 4 hours, until dry to the touch. Remove from oven and allow to air-dry in a cool dry place for another 24 hours.

- Store in a covered container or zip-top bag.

## CHEF'S NOTE

*The Dothraki are a brutal, nomadic race who depend on the equine world for survival, in fact Dothraki literally means riders. As well as depending on horses to travel, their meat is the main part of the Dothraki diet, along with fermented mare's milk. This jerky may be beef but it has plenty of horse power.*

# Meat & Onion Skewers

## Serves 8

**For the skewers**
- 3 tbsp fresh chopped coriander
- 300g/11oz Sirloin or rump steaks, cut into 3-4cm chunks
- 10 spring onions
- 1 tbsp toasted sesame oil
- Vegetable oil for brushing
- Sesame seeds to sprinkle

**For the marinade**
- 4 tbsp mirin
- 4 tbsp tamari or soy sauce
- 4 tbsp chicken stock or rice wine
- 2 tsp freshly grated ginger
- 1 garlic clove, crushed
- ½ tsp chilli flakes
- 2 tsp sugar
- Juice 1 lime
- 8 bamboo skewers soaked in water

## METHOD

- Put all of the marinade ingredients in a bowl and stir to dissolve the sugar.

- Add the beef and mix to coat. Set aside for at least 1 hour.

- Cut the spring onions in half, then slice in half lengthways. Brush with the sesame oil and set aside.

- When ready to cook, heat a griddle pan. Divide the beef among the skewers and nestle spring onions between the chunks (keep the marinade).

- Brush the meat with vegetable oil and griddle for 2-3 minutes on each side, turning, until cooked to your liking.

- Meanwhile, put the reserved marinade in a small pan and bubble for 5 minutes over a high heat until reduced and syrupy.

- Serve the skewers drizzled with the reduced marinade and sprinkled with sesame seeds and coriander leaves.

## CHEF'S NOTE

*When on her way to The Eyrie, Catelyn Stark dines on the most delicious sounding meal when she is offered skewers of charred meat and onions still hot from the spit. Catelyn had not realised how hungry she was. She ate standing in the yard, as stablehands moved their saddles to fresh mules. The hot juices ran down her chin and dripped onto her cloak, but she was too famished to care.*

# Stick Them With The Pointy End

### Serves 8

## INGREDIENTS

- 4 chicken mini-fillets
- 1 tbsp soy sauce
- 1 orange, zest only
- 2 tbsp olive oil
- 8 mini wooden skewers, soaked in water for ten minutes

## METHOD

- Slice each mini-fillet in half lengthways and place in a small bowl.

- Add the soy sauce, orange zest and olive oil. Leave to marinade for as long as possible.

- Thread each chicken mini-fillet onto a skewer. Heat a griddle pan and fry the chicken skewers for three minutes on each side, or until cooked through. Serve immediately.

## ◄ CHEF'S NOTE ►

*Arya certainly took heed of Jon's parting words of wisdom and has stuck plenty of people with the pointy end of her sword 'Needle'. In fact she's become quite the baby-faced killer.*

# Molten Gold Crown Dip

## Serves 6

### INGREDIENTS

- 1 tbsp unsalted butter
- 1 tbsp plain flour
- 120ml/4floz milk (plus more if needed during cooking)
- 175g/6oz grated cheddar or Red Leicester cheese
- Pinch of salt and cayenne pepper

## METHOD

- Melt the butter in a small saucepan over medium heat.

- Add the flour and cook for 1 minute, stirring constantly.

- Whisk in half of the milk and cook until slightly thickened. Then gradually add the rest of the milk and cook until you get a creamy sauce – about 1-3mins.

- Turn heat to low and stir in the cheese until smooth and all of the cheese is melted.

- You may add more milk if the consistency is too thick.

- Season to taste with salt and cayenne pepper.

### ◄ CHEF'S NOTE ►

*Viserys Targaryen was a cruel and arrogant man, caught up in his belief that he'd been denied his birth right as the King's heir to the throne, of ruling the Seven Kingdoms. He partially got his wish when Khal Drogo gave him 'a golden crown that men will tremble to behold' and poured molten gold on his head. Thank the many-faced God!*

# Bread & Salt

## Serves 12

## INGREDIENTS

- 450g/1lb strong white bread flour, plus extra for dusting
- 1 x 7g/⅛oz sachet fast-action dried yeast
- 1½ tsp salt
- 250ml/8½ floz warm water
- Vegetable oil or spray oil
- 2 tbsp extra virgin olive oil
- 4 tbsp sea salt

## METHOD

- Dust two large baking trays with flour.

- Put the flour, yeast and the salt into a large bowl and add enough of the water to form a soft dough. Knead well for 10 minutes by hand on a lightly floured work surface.

- Divide the mixture into 12 equal portions, each weighing about 60g/2½oz. Roll the portions into balls, then place each ball on a floured surface and roll into a long sausage shape about 25cmx2cm/10inx1in.

- Place the breadsticks on the prepared baking trays, spacing them 4cm/1½in apart.

- Cover the breadsticks loosely with oiled cling film, making sure it is airtight.

- Leave in a warm place for 30 minutes, or until the breadsticks have almost doubled in size.

- Preheat the oven to 200C/400F/Gas 6.

- Unwrap the clingfilm and brush all the breadsticks with the extra virgin olive oil. Sprinkle the breadsticks with the sea salt.

- Bake on the top third of the oven for about 20 minutes, or until the breadsticks are lightly golden-brown and feel firm to the touch. Remove the breadsticks from the oven and leave to cool on the baking trays.

## ◄ CHEF'S NOTE ►

*Bread and salt is a key part of Westerosi culture and 'guest right'. When a guest eats the food off a host's table beneath the host's roof, the 'guest right' is invoked. Once invoked, neither the guest can harm his host nor the host harm his guest for the length of the guest's stay.*
*These breadsticks are delicious when served with the molten gold crown dip (see p14).*

# Show The Fig

## Serves 24

- 2 sheets filo pastry (measuring 25x25cm /10x10in square)
- 55g/2oz unsalted butter, melted
- 3 ripe figs
- 100g/3½oz Roquefort (or similar blue raw milk sheep's cheese)
- 1 tsp lemon juice
- 3 chopped sage leaves
- A sprinkling of ground paprika

## METHOD

- Preheat the oven to 200C/400F/Gas 6.

- Brush two sheets of filo with butter, place on top of each other and cut into 24 equal squares.

- Put the squares together in pairs on top of each other at a 45 degree angle to make a star shape. Press into the holes of 2 x 12 mini-muffin tin. Repeat with the remaining pastry to make 24 mini tartlets.

- Bake in the oven for 5-10mins, or until golden-brown and crisp.

- Chop the figs into small pieces, and divide between the cooked filo cases. Put the cheese, lemon juice and sage into a bowl.

- Mash with a fork, season with pepper, then spoon blobs of cheese mixture on top of the fig. Sprinkle lightly with paprika.

- Bake in the oven for five minutes, or until the cheese has just melted.

## ◄ CHEF'S NOTE ►

*Showing someone the fig is the Westerosi version of flipping the bird. A rude gesture based on a Roman sign that is still used today in Turkish and Slavic cultures, so called because it resembles a fig, or a rather rude part of a woman's anatomy. There's no fear of your guests being so rude after they've eaten these tasty tarts!*

# Night King Spears

## Serves 10

- 150g/5oz ready-made puff pastry
- Flour for dusting
- 50g/2oz cream cheese
- 10 asparagus spears
- 1 beaten egg
- 2 tbsp grated parmesan

## METHOD

- Preheat the oven to 200C/400F/Gas 6.

- Roll the pastry out on a floured surface into a 15cmx25cm/6inx10in rectangle and spread all over with the cream cheese.

- Using a sharp knife, cut the pastry into 10 long, thin strips.

- Wrap one pastry strip in a spiral around each asparagus spear and place onto a baking tray. Lightly brush each with the beaten egg then scatter over the parmesan.

- Bake the spears in the oven for 15-20mins, or until the pastry has risen and is golden brown.

## ◄ CHEF'S NOTE ►

*Who knew until the last series that the Night King was hiding his Olympic level javelin throwing skills? Go for gold by serving with the molten crown dip (see p14).*

# Mini Hot Pies

## Serves 8

### INGREDIENTS

- 500g/1lb 2oz pack shortcrust pastry
- 2 cooked chicken breasts, shredded
- 75g/3oz frozen peas
- 4 asparagus spears trimmed and cut into bite-size pieces
- 100g/3½oz crème fraîche
- 1 beaten egg

## METHOD

- Roll out the pastry until a little thinner than a £1 coin.

- Cut out 8x9cm circles and use to line 8 holes of a muffin tin. Divide chicken, peas and asparagus between holes, season, and then place 1tbsp crème fraiche over.

- Cut out 8x7cm circles to make tops for the pies. Lightly brush edges of the pie bases with egg, place each top onto its pie and press down into the filling.

- Pinch together the sides to seal. Leave to rest in the fridge for 30 mins.

- Heat oven to 200C/400F/Gas 6.

- Brush tops with more egg and bake the pies for 30-35mins or until the pastry is crisp and golden. Serve warm.

---

### ◄┤ CHEF'S NOTE ├►

*Hot Pie is one of the few characters who seems to have achieved his goals and had a happy ending. An orphaned baker's apprentice who dreamed of being able to bake. These mini-pies are fit to grace his menu at The Inn at the Crossroads.*

# Oberyn's Smashed Potatoes

### Serves 10

## INGREDIENTS

- 1kg/2lbs 4oz new potatoes
- A light spray/brush of olive oil
- 3 tbsp melted butter
- 4 crushed cloves of garlic
- 1 tbsp fresh chopped parsley
- Salt and black pepper to taste
- 2 tbsp parmesan cheese

## METHOD

- Place the potatoes in a large pot of salted water. Bring to the boil; cook, covered for 30-35mins or until just tender. Drain well.

- Pre-heat the grill.

- Lightly grease a large baking sheet with cooking spray. Arrange potatoes onto the sheet and use a potato masher to lightly flatten the potatoes.

- Mix together the butter, garlic and parsley. Pour the mixture over each potato. Sprinkle with salt and pepper and lightly spray/brush with the oil spray.

- Grill the potatoes until they are golden and crispy (about 10-15mins).

- Remove from the oven, sprinkle over the parmesan cheese and return to the heat until the cheese is melted.

- To serve, season with a little extra salt and parsley and some pointy cocktail sticks to skewer them with.

## ◄ CHEF'S NOTE ►

*Obreyn Martell was a feisty, hot blooded Dornish fighter who came soooooo close to escaping combat with The Mountain before his head ended up crushed like a smashed potato.*

# Mini
# Ned's Heads

## Serves 18

### INGREDIENTS

- 450g/1lb minced chicken
- ½ onion finely sliced
- 3 tbsp breadcrumbs
- 1 egg
- ½ tsp cayenne pepper
- 2 tbsp olive oil
- 250ml/8½floz BBQ sauce
- Salt

## METHOD

- Mix the chicken, onion, breadcrumbs, egg and cayenne with a little salt and pepper.

- Use your hands to shape into 1-inch balls.

- In large pan heat the olive oil and cook the meatballs in over medium-high heat until browned and cooked through.

- Stir in the BBQ sauce and cook for a further 2mins until everything is piping hot.

- Thread a meatball onto a skewer and serve with dressing.

## ◄ CHEF'S NOTE ►

*Back at the beginning of the series we didn't know what a psychopathic sadist George R.R. Martin was, we grew to love Ned Stark as the series' moral center. His beheading and the impalement of his head was one of Game of Thrones most shocking moments, but it did inspire these bloody meatballs on sticks, so every cloud…*

# Oat-h Keeper Canapes

## Serves 6

- ½ Arbroath smokie or smoked salmon fillet skinned, boned and flaked into small pieces
- 2 tbsp Greek yoghurt
- 1 tbsp chopped fresh dill
- 1 tbsp chopped fresh chives
- Juice of ½ lemon
- 6 small oatcakes
- 6 thin slices of cucumber
- 1 ripe tomato, chopped and seeds removed
- Freshly ground black pepper

## METHOD

- First make the pâté by placing the fish, yoghurt and herbs into a bowl and mashing together with a fork until really well combined.

- Spread some of the pâté onto each of the oatcakes.

- Top with the cucumber, chopped tomato, a drop of lemon juice and plenty of black pepper.

### ◀ CHEF'S NOTE ▶

*Brienne of Tarth is a total badass, fighting and killing with more strength than most men in her desire to uphold her oath to Catelyn Stark. Her skills win over Jamie Lannister who gifts her Ned Stark's former sword, forged from Valyrian steel which she dubbed 'Oathkeeper'.*

# Blood & Cheese

## Serves 24

## INGREDIENTS

- 2 x sheets of filo pastry (48x25cm/ 19x10in)
- 50g/2oz unsalted butter, melted
- 150g/5oz brie
- 2 tsp wholegrain mustard
- 100g/3½oz cranberry sauce
- 75g/3oz smoked back bacon rashers, cut into 1cm/½in strips
- Freshly ground black pepper

## METHOD

- Preheat the oven to 190C/370F/Gas 5.

- Take one half of a sheet of pastry and brush it with a little of the melted butter.

- Cut this half into 20 rough 5cm/2in squares. Take three of the squares and place them on top of each other, placing each at a slight angle to the one underneath (forming a star shape).

- Push the stack of pastry squares into one of the holes of mini muffin tins, to make an empty pastry case. Repeat with the remaining pastry until all 24 holes are filled.

- Cut the brie into 24 small pieces and place one piece into each partially cooked pastry case.

- Dot with a little mustard, add cranberry sauce and top with a few strips of bacon.

- Bake for 10–12 minutes, or until the bacon is cooked, the cheese melted and the pastry golden-brown.

- Leave to cool in the tin for a couple of minutes before removing carefully and serving.

### ◄ CHEF'S NOTE ►

*Way back in Game of Thrones lore, Blood & Cheese were hitmen and rat-catchers, hired to bump off Aegon II Targaryen's sons and heirs to the Iron Throne. This brutal event may come back to have significance with recent revelations about Jon Snow's ancestry.*

# Milk Of The Poppy

## Serves 10

### INGREDIENTS

- 75g/3oz parmesan, finely grated
- 1 tsp poppy seeds
- 1 tsp sesame seeds
- Butter, for greasing
- 10 lollypop sticks

## METHOD

- Preheat the oven to 220C/425F/Gas 7, line two large baking trays with baking paper and grease them with butter.

- Mix the cheese and seeds together in a small bowl. Sit a 9cm/3½in chefs' ring or cookie cutter on one of the baking trays and sprinkle a small handful of the cheese mixture into it, in a thin layer. Carefully lift the ring off to reveal a neat-edged disc of parmesan and lay a lollipop stick on top, with the tip of the stick touching the middle of the disc.

- Repeat with the remaining cheese and sticks to make 10 in total (leaving about 3cm/1¼in spaces between them to allow for any spreading during cooking).

- You should have a little parmesan left over, so use it to cover up the part of the lollipop stick resting on the disc.

- Bake in the oven for five minutes, swapping the lollipops to a different shelf halfway through. The cheese should be lightly golden-brown and bubbling.

- Remove from the oven and slide the paper off the baking trays and onto a rack to help speed up cooling. Leave to cool for 1–2 minutes, or until the lollipops have become crisp. Very carefully remove each one with a palette knife.

## CHEF'S NOTE

*Both painkiller and anaesthetic, milk of the poppy is a powerful substance made by maesters from crushed poppy flowers and used throughout the Seven Kingdoms. When consumed to excess it's highly addictive, much like eating these cheesy lollypops.*

# STARK FAMILY STARTERS

# Dornish Salad

## Serves 6

## INGREDIENTS

**For the dressing**
- 6 tbsp blood-orange juice (roughly the juice of 1 or 2 blood oranges)
- 1 tbsp pomegranate molasses
- 6 tbsp extra-virgin olive oil
- 2 tsp runny honey

**For the salad**
- 5 blood oranges
- 1 large fennel bulb
- 125g/4oz watercress
- About 30 black olives
- 2 balls of good quality mozzarella
- Extra-virgin olive oil for drizzling

## METHOD

Whisk the dressing ingredients along with some salt and pepper to season to your taste.

Slice the bottom and top off each orange so they sit flat. Using a sharp knife, cut off the rind and pith in strips, slicing from top to bottom and working your way around each orange. Slice the flesh horizontally, removing any seeds.

Quarter the fennel and remove the coarser outer leaves. Trim off the fronds from the top and keep them for the salad.

Remove the core from each quarter and then cut very finely (wafer-like is best) preferably using a mandolin.

Carefully toss the fennel, watercress, olives and dressing.

Drain the mozzarella and, just before serving, tear into pieces. Put on top of the salad. Drizzle with the olive oil and grind on some black pepper.

## ◄ CHEF'S NOTE ►

*As the hottest land in the Seven Kingdoms, Dorne is home to fantastic produce not found anywhere else including; olives, pomegranate and blood orange. This dish is a celebration of Dornish delights.*

# The Onion Knight Soup

## Serves 6

## INGREDIENTS

- 50g/2oz butter
- 1kg/2lb 4oz onions, thinly sliced
- 2 garlic cloves, chopped
- 100ml/3½floz white wine
- 2 tbsp Madeira, plus extra once cooked, to taste
- 1lt/1½pts fresh beef stock
- Salt and freshly ground black pepper

## METHOD

- Melt the butter in a medium-sized pan, add the onions and garlic and gently fry over a low heat for 30-35 minutes, stirring occasionally, until the onions are really soft and a rich dark brown colour.

- Add the white wine, stirring the bottom of the pan to loosen the browned onion.

- Bring it back to the boil then add the Madeira and beef stock.

- Bring to the boil and then lower the heat and simmer for about 10-12 mins.

- Taste the soup to check the seasoning, and add salt and freshly ground black pepper to taste.

- Add another few tablespoons of Madeira to the soup, to boost the flavour and stir well.

- Serve ladled into bowls with fresh bread on the side.

## ◄ CHEF'S NOTE ►

*Ser Davos Seaworth or the Onion Knight is a loyal and trusted advisor first, to Stannis Baratheon and then to Jon Snow. A reformed smuggler, it was his bounty of onions that allowed Stannis' army to survive Robert's Rebellion, earning him a knighthood and his nickname!*

# Green Salad With Apple & Pine Nuts

## Serves 6

### INGREDIENTS

- 250g/9oz cos lettuce
- 250g/9oz baby spinach
- 150g/5oz toasted pinenuts
- 5 apples
- 250g/9oz goat's cheese
- 2 tsp balsamic vinegar
- 2 tbsp honey

## METHOD

- Combine the lettuce and spinach and divide between 6 plates.

- Slice the apples into thin rounds coring as you go but don't peel.

- Stack these on top of the greens- alternating colours, and sprinkling a little cheese in between.

- Top with a bit of cheese and a sprinkle of nuts.

- Mix the honey and balsamic well then pour over the salads and serve.

### ◄ CHEF'S NOTE ►

*'Cersei set a tasty table, that could not be denied. They started with a creamy chestnut soup, crusty hot bread, and greens dressed with apples and pine nuts.' Like Cersei this salad has a bitter edge, and is quite nutty!*

# Olenna Tyrell's Cheese

### Serves 4-6

## INGREDIENTS

- 200g/7oz wheel of brie or camembert
- 1 tbsp honey, for drizzling
- Fresh rosemary leaves
- 4 apples, cored & sliced
- 1 crust baguette

## METHOD

- Drizzle the cheese with honey and top with rosemary.

- Bake at 170C/350F/Gas 4 until soft and starting to ooze - this should take around 10mins.

- Serve with apples slices and crusty bread.

### CHEF'S NOTE

*Olenna Tyrell's servant should have known better than to try and tell her that cheese should be served after desert. A queen has cheese served when she wants it served!!*

# Tales Of Duck & Egg

## Serves 4

## INGREDIENTS

- 1 tbsp butter
- 6 spring onions, chopped
- 75g/3oz chopped ham
- 4 tbsp double cream
- 2 tbsp crushed croutons
- 4 duck eggs
- Toasted baguette, to serve

## METHOD

- Preheat the oven to 160C/325F/Gas 3. Heat the butter in a small pan and fry the spring onions until crispy.

- Add the ham and cook for another minute. Remove and drain on a paper towel.

- Divide the ham and spring onions between four ramekins, then add the croutons, pour in the cream and season well.

- Break an egg into each ramekin. Place the ramekins in a deep roasting tin, then pour in boiling water until it reaches half-way up the side of each ramekin.

- Bake for 10-12mins, or until firm. Serve immediately with toasted bread.

## ◄• CHEF'S NOTE •►

*The end is nigh for fans of the Game of Thrones television series, and book fans may have given up hope of ever seeing it finished. But the worlds of A Song of Ice and Fire, can still be enjoyed- Tales of Duck & Egg are fantastic escapism for those going through withdrawals.*

# Dragon Fire Chicken Wings

## Serves 6

### INGREDIENTS

- 4 tbsp tomato ketchup
- 4 garlic cloves, crushed
- 6 tbsp honey
- 6 tbsp soy sauce
- 2 tsp crushed chilli flakes
- 2 tbsp Dijon mustard
- 1.5kg/3lb 6oz chicken wings

## METHOD

- Mix together the ketchup, garlic, honey, soy, chilli & mustard to make a marinade.

- Add the chicken and marinade in a ziplock bag in the fridge for at least 2 hours.

- Heat the oven to 180C/350F/Gas 6. Line a roasting tin with a double layer of foil.

- Arrange the chicken and all the marinade in a single layer and roast for 35-40mins, or until browned and bubbling, basting half way through cooking.

- Sprinkle over some sea salt and black pepper and serve.

## ◀ CHEF'S NOTE ▶

*Drogon, Rhaegal, and Viserion are Daenerys' fearsome dragons, hatched from fire and named after her dead husband and brothers. These wings may not have seen the flames but they definitely have heat!*

# Brienne's Bacon Wrapped Trout

## Serves 6

### INGREDIENTS

- 6 trout fillets (or any firm white fish will do)
- 6 strips thick cut bacon
- 1 tbsp olive oil
- Juice of 1 lemon
- 2 sprigs thyme
- Green salad to serve

### METHOD

- Season the fish and sprinkle with thyme leaves.

- Squeeze the lemon over the fillets.

- Wrap each fish in the bacon and fry in a hot pan with a little oil for around 3mins a side or until the bacon is crispy.

- Serve immediately with a green salad garnish.

### ◄ CHEF'S NOTE ►

*'She stared at the supper set before her: trout wrapped in bacon, salad of turnip greens and sweetgrass, pease and onions and hot bread. Brienne was eating methodically, as if supper were a chore to be accomplished.' Brienne of Tarth is too focused on fulfilling her oath to give much thought to food, but if she'd tasted trout from this recipe, she might have changed her mind!*

# Tywin's Cross-Bow Steak

## Serves 4

## INGREDIENTS

- 400g/14oz cross cut blade or beef rump steaks
- 75g/3oz baby spinach leaves, washed

**For the dressing**

- 2 tbsp freshly chopped coriander leaves
- 2 tbsp lime juice
- 1tbsp sunflower oil
- 1 garlic clove, crushed
- 1 red chilli, finely chopped

## METHOD

- Season the beef with salt and freshly ground black pepper.

- Heat a large frying pan and sear the beef over high heat until it is cooked but still pink. This will take about 2mins a side. Set aside at room temperature.

- Meanwhile, make the dressing by combining all of the ingredients in a small bowl.

- Thinly slice the beef and arrange it on the spinach leaves.

- Spoon over the dressing and serve.

## CHEF'S NOTE

*Tywin Lannister was the power-hungry and manipulative glue that held the Lannister clan together. His scheming and backstabbing finally saw him come a cropper when Tyrion robbed him of his life and dignity-shooting him with a crossbow whilst on the privy.*

# Beef & Barley Broth

## Serves 6-8

## INGREDIENTS

- 1 large knob of butter
- 1 tsp olive oil
- 500g/1lb 2oz diced stewing steak
- 1 tbsp Marmite
- 1 splash of Worcestershire sauce
- 1 red onion
- 2 carrots
- 3 sticks of celery
- 1 fresh bay leaf
- 1 sprig of fresh rosemary
- 1 tbsp plain flour
- 2l/3pts beef stock
- 150g/5oz pearl barley

## METHOD

Melt the butter in a large pan over a medium heat, add a splash of olive oil and the steak, and cook until the meat is lightly browned all over.

Stir in the Marmite and Worcestershire sauce, turn the heat up to high and keep stirring until all the liquid has evaporated.

Meanwhile, peel and/or trim and chop the onion, carrots and celery.

Add the chopped veg to the pan with the bay leaf and rosemary sprig and cook over a low heat with the lid on until softened.

Stir in the flour and, after 1 minute, pour in the stock. Season well with sea salt and black pepper.

Bring to the boil, then reduce to a simmer, add the pearl barley and cook gently for 1 hour, then remove from the heat and discard the rosemary sprig (if you like) and bay leaf.

Blend the soup with a stick blender until it reaches a consistency you like.

Serve with fresh bread.

## ⊰ CHEF'S NOTE ⊱

*Beef and barley stew is a classic dish in Westeros, beloved by travellers and enjoyed by Bran Stark. This is exactly the sort of dish to keep you warm in The North, particularly when winter is coming.*

# Bran's Bedside Breakfast

## Serves 6

### INGREDIENTS

- 6 quail's eggs (or any smallish eggs will do)
- 6 strips of bacon
- A slice of bread
- Butter, honey, and berry preserves
- 6 small slices of cheddar

## METHOD

- Fry the bacon in a hot pan for a few minutes until crispy and then drain excess fat on a slice of kitchen roll.

- Boil the quails eggs by placing in boiling water for 3 mins.

- Whilst they're cooking toast a slice of bread then butter and cut into 6 soldiers.

- Serve on 6 plates, each with one egg, one piece of bacon and a slice of toast.

- Place honey and jam on the table for guests to help themselves.

---

### ◄ CHEF'S NOTE ►

*'There was much more than she'd asked for: hot bread, butter and honey and blackberry preserves, a rasher of bacon and a soft-boiled egg, a wedge of cheese, a pot of mint tea.' This mini breakfast plays tribute to the one dined upon by Catelyn Stark when at Bran's bedside.*

# Qyburn's Experiment

## Serves 6

## INGREDIENTS

- 3 fresh chorizo sausages, sliced into rounds the thickness of a pound coin
- 4 spring onions, trimmed and sliced
- 2 red chillies, thickly sliced
- 24 scallops, cleaned (with 6 shells reserved and cleaned if you can get them)
- 2 tbsp runny honey

## METHOD

- Heat a heavy griddle pan over a high heat.

- Fry the chorizo until it is browned and some of the juices are running into the pan.

- Add the spring onion and chilli and fry for 2-3mins.

- Add the scallops and fry for 2-3 minutes on either side or until cooked through.

- Drizzle over the runny honey and stir to coat.

- Divide the scallops and chorizo among the six scallop shells and serve.

## ◄ CHEF'S NOTE ►

*Former maester Qyburn is an odd fellow. A skilled healer, but something of the psychopath conducting Frankenstein-esq experiments. The idea of fish and pork may seem odd but like Qyburn's experiments, it works fantastically well.*

# Little Birds

## Serves 6

## INGREDIENTS

- 6 quail
- 2 garlic cloves, finely sliced
- 5cm/2in piece fresh ginger, finely grated
- 1 tsp chilli powder
- 1 tsp ground fennel seed
- ½ tsp ground cinnamon
- 1 tsp garam masala
- 200ml/7floz natural yoghurt, plus 6tbsp for serving

## METHOD

Begin by preparing the quail. Do this by using some strong, sharp scissors to cut down either side of the spine. Take out the spine then press down on the breastbone of the quail to open it out flat. Cut the quail in half lengthways.

Make the marinade by mixing the spices and yoghurt in a bowl until well combined.

Coat the quail with the marinade, cover with cling film and chill in the fridge for at least 2 hours.

When ready to eat, heat a griddle pan until hot, then add the quail, skin-side down, and cook for 5-6 minutes on each side, or until the quail is cooked through and juices run clear when a skewer is inserted into the thickest part.

Remove the quail from the griddle and leave to rest for 2-3 minutes.

Serve with a tbsp of yoghurt and some flatbread.

## ◄ CHEF'S NOTE ►

*Varys is known as The Spider for the web of influence he's able to weave, obtaining secrets from across the Seven Kingdoms and trading them as his sees fit. Aided by his Little Birds, he's hoping to keep the world safe from the wrong hands.*

# Baratheon Stag

## Serves 6

## INGREDIENTS

- 12 shallots (unpeeled)
- 2 tbsp olive oil, plus extra for brushing
- 1 sprig of fresh thyme
- 1kg/2¼lb boned venison loin
- 2 tbsp grated fresh horseradish
- 200ml/7floz crème fraîche
- 1 tsp white wine vinegar
- 1 sprig of fresh rosemary
- Zest of 1 orange

## METHOD

- Preheat the oven to 180°C/350°F/Gas 4.

- Toss the shallots in olive oil, season and place in a baking dish with the thyme sprig.

- Cover tightly with foil and bake in the oven for 45mins or until soft.

- Meanwhile, preheat a large frying pan.

- Remove all the fat and any sinew from the venison, season well, and brush with olive oil.

- Place in the hot pan and cook for a few minutes each size (or to your taste). Place on a plate to cool for about 30mins.

- Mix the horseradish into the crème fraîche. Season it well with salt, pepper and the vinegar.

- Finely chop the rosemary and finely grate the zest of the orange.

- Thinly slice the venison with a sharp carving knife and lay 3 slices on each plate.

- Peel some of the warm shallots, tear them in half and lay on top of each piece of venison. Spoon a little horseradish crème fraîche on top and sprinkle the plates with the rosemary and orange zest before serving.

## ◄ CHEF'S NOTE ►

*Members of The House of Baratheon have dropped like flies since the beginning of the series with Robert, Joffrey, Renley, Stannis and poor Tommen and Myrcella all biting the dust. Eat this delicious venison in remembrance of a once great house.*

# Dothra-quiche

## Serves 6

## INGREDIENTS

- 350g/12oz ready-made shortcrust pastry
- Plain flour, for dusting
- 4 medium free-eggs, beaten
- 150ml/5floz whole milk
- 200g/7oz sandwich pickle, preferably Branston (small chunks)
- 250g/9oz mature Cheddar cheese, grated

## METHOD

Preheat the oven to 180°C/350°F/Gas 4 and put a baking tray in to heat up.

Dust the work surface with a little flour and roll the pastry into a circle that will easily cover a 23cm/9in tin, about the thickness of a pound coin. Lay the pastry over the tin and press it into the edges, right into the grooves, leaving some overhanging.

Line the pastry with baking paper and fill with ceramic baking beans to cover the base.

Put the lined tin on the preheated baking tray and bake in the oven for 25 minutes. Remove the paper and the baking beans and return to the oven for 15 minutes, until cooked through and golden-brown.

Meanwhile, mix the eggs in a jug with the milk.

Spread the base of the tart shell with sandwich pickle over the base, sprinkle over the grated cheese evenly and pour in the egg mixture. Put the whole tray back in the oven on the middle shelf to cook for 25–30mins or until the filling is set with just a very slight wobble in the middle.

Once the tart has cooled enough to handle, trim off the excess pastry using a sharp serrated knife. Leave to cool in the tin for 30 minutes, then transfer to a wire rack.

Slice and serve.

## ◀ CHEF'S NOTE ▶

*The Dothraki screamers are fearsome fighters, known as Horselords who are born, fight and then die in the saddle. This tasty quiche is exactly the kind of protein punch the clan could have done with before a heavy night of battles and raids.*

# Ser Jorah's Humble Pie

## Serves 12

## INGREDIENTS

**For the pastry**
- 250g/9oz strong white bread flour
- 60g/2¼oz lard
- 60g/2¼oz salted butter
- 100ml/3½floz iced water
- 1 free-range egg, beaten with 2 tsp milk, to glaze

**For the filling**
- 125g/4oz beef skirt steak, cut into small cubes
- 100g/3½oz waxy potatoes, such as Charlotte, peeled and finely diced
- 60g/2¼oz swede, peeled and finely diced
- 60g/2¼oz onion, finely diced
- Sea salt and freshly ground black pepper

## METHOD

- Combine the flour, lard and butter in a large bowl and gently rub together with your fingertips until the mixture resembles fine breadcrumbs.

- Gradually work in enough water to bring the mixture together to form a smooth dough.

- Turn out onto a clean work surface and knead into a smooth ball. Flatten out into a disc, wrap in cling film and put in the fridge for 2 hours until firm.

- Meanwhile, combine the ingredients for the filling in a bowl and season with salt and plenty of black pepper.

- Preheat the oven to 180°C/350°F/Gas 4 and line a baking tray with baking paper.

- Roll out the dough to the thickness of a pound coin and use a 10cm/4in cookie cutter to cut out 12 circles of pastry.

- Divide the mixture between the circles, fold the pastry in half, and then crimp the edges to seal.

- Brush the pasties with the glaze, transfer to the lined baking sheets and bake for 30 minutes, or until golden.

## ◄ CHEF'S NOTE ►

*A lesson to all of us in how you can't make someone love you no matter what you do. Ser Jorah Mormont has been well and truly taught the art of friend zoning by Dany. She may have let him back into the fold after he'd eaten some humble pie, but no matter what he does he can't compete with Jon Snow when it comes to the Mother of Dragon's affections.*

# Braavos Seafood Feast

## Serves 6

## INGREDIENTS

**For the salmon pâté**
- 200g/7oz smoked salmon trimmings
- 100g/3½oz cream cheese
- 75g/3oz soured cream/crème fraîche
- ½ lemon, juice and grated zest
- 1 cucumber cut into slices
- 24 crostini or mini Melba toasts

**For the prawns**
- 250g/9oz cooked, peeled king prawns
- 1 lemon, juice only
- Small bunch flat leaf parsley, chopped

**For the blinis**
- 36 canapé blinis
- 100g/3½oz smoked salmon trimmings
- 75ml/2½floz soured cream
- 1 x 50g jar lumpfish caviar
- ½ lemon, for squeezing
- 150g/5oz good-quality mayonnaise

## METHOD

For the smoked salmon pâté, put the salmon, cream cheese, soured cream, lemon juice & black pepper in a food processor and blend until you have a rough paste. Transfer to a serving bowl. Refrigerate for an hour.

Shortly before serving, put the prawns into a bowl and squeeze over the lemon juice. Arrange the lemony prawns in a serving bowl, sprinkle with parsley & season with salt and pepper. Serve the mayonnaise alongside for dipping.

Immediately before serving, heat the oven to 180°C/350°F/Gas 4. Place the blinis on a tray and heat in the oven for 5 minutes. Meanwhile warm a serving plate.

Cut the salmon trimmings into pieces ready to top the blinis.

Remove the blinis from the oven and transfer to the warmed serving plate and apoon ½ tsp of soured cream on each blini.

Add a little smoked salmon to the top of 18 of the blinis and a quarter of a teaspoon of caviar onto the remaining 18. Squeeze a little lemon over and serve with ground black pepper if you have it.

To serve the smoked salmon pâté garnish with the cucumber slices and serve spread on mini toasts.

## ◀ CHEF'S NOTE ▶

*Braavos is the northern-most and richest of the Free Cities. Home to the famous Iron Bank, wealth is abundant and attitudes are free and liberal. With two main harbours it is famous for its seafood. This seafood feast is a wonderful display of Braavos' treasures and decadence.*

# Mains
# Fit for the
# Mountain

# Robert's Revenge

## Serves 6

## INGREDIENTS

- 700g/1lb 9oz boneless wild boar (or pork shoulder will do)
- 5 tbsp vegetable oil
- 4 rashers smoked streaky bacon or pancetta, cut into 1cm slices
- 1 large onion, finely chopped
- 4 garlic cloves, crushed
- 75g/3oz pitted black olives, rinsed & drained
- 500ml/2 cups red wine
- 1 tin chopped tomatoes
- 2 tbsp tomato puree
- 500ml/2 cups beef stock
- 2 large bay leaves
- 3 sprigs of thyme
- 1 rosemary stalk

## METHOD

- Cut the meat into chunky pieces. Trim off any excessive fat and eason well.

- Heat 2 tbsp of the oil in a large frying pan and fry the meat in batches over a medium-high heat until browned on all sides. Transfer into a casserole dish or lidded saucepan.

- Add a little more oil to the frying pan and fry the bacon until crispy, then scatter it over the boar/pork.

- Fry the chopped onion in the same pan over a low heat for 5 minutes or until softened. Add the garlic & olives and cook for 2 minutes more, stirring.

- Add them to the meat in the casserole dish, then pour in the wine. Stir in the tomatoes, tomato puree and beef stock. Add all the herbs and bring the mixture to a simmer.

- Stir well, cover loosely with a lid and leave the to simmer very gently for 2½ hours, or until the meat is very tender.

- Stir occasionally adding a little extra water if needed.

- Remove the thyme, rosemary stalks & bay leaves, then season to taste. Serve with freshly cooked pasta and grated Parmesan.

## CHEF'S NOTE

*A wild boar (with a little help from Cersei) may have ended King Robert Baratheon's life and thrown life in Westeros into a chaotic bloodbath, but we can take revenge upon the savage beast and celebrate the fact that without him we'd have no Game of Thrones.*

# The Hound's Roast Chicken

## Serves 4

## INGREDIENTS

- 1 large chicken (approx. 1½kg/3lb 6oz)
- 1 lemon
- 2 tbsp butter
- Sea salt flakes

## METHOD

- Preheat the oven to 220C/425F/Gas 7.

- Cut the lemon in half and scatter a little salt over the cut side before placing inside the chicken's cavity

- Spread the butter underneath the skin of the chicken and then place it in the oven for 1½hrs or until the skin is crispy and the juices run clear when a skewer is inserted into the fattest part (a 1½kg chicken will take 90 mins in the oven, a larger chicken will take longer).

- Remove the chicken from the oven, squeeze the juice from the remaining lemon half over the chicken and sprinkle some salt. Serve with Lannister Golden Potatoes (see p46) and steamed greens.

## ◄ CHEF'S NOTE ►

*Perhaps the only thing The Hound would love more than one of these roast chickens, is two of these roast chickens. When Polliver and other of the Mountain's men refuse Sandor Clegane's demand for a chicken it was only a matter of time before carnage ensued.*

# Lannister Golden Potatoes

### Serves 4

## INGREDIENTS

- 6 even-sized medium potatoes
- 4 tbsp rapeseed oil
- 2 tsp chopped rosemary
- Sea salt flakes

## METHOD

- Put the whole unpeeled potatoes in a pan of water.

- Bring to the boil and cook for 15 mins. Drain and leave to cool.

- When ready to serve, strip the skins from the potatoes, then cut them into thick slices.

- Heat the oil in a very large non-stick frying pan.

- Add the potatoes in a single layer if there is room, and cook for 10-15 mins, turning them frequently with a fish slice until they are golden & crispy on the outside and tender on the inside.

- Sprinkle with the rosemary and flaky salt to serve.

## ◄ CHEF'S NOTE ►

*The Lannisters always pay their debts. They've built a powerful dynasty propped up by former wealth and the Iron Bank of Braavos following the depletion of their last gold mine some years ago. These potatoes resemble the Lannister's golden coins and make an excellent accompaniment to The Hound's roast chicken or Tyrion's leg of lamb.*

# Wildling Stew

## Serves 4

## INGREDIENTS

- 750g/1lb 11oz lamb neck fillet, cut into 2.5cm/1in cubes
- Salt and freshly ground black pepper
- 25g/1oz plain flour
- 1 tbsp olive oil
- 50g/2oz butter
- 12 shallots, peeled
- 2 medium carrots, cut into large dice
- 1 medium swede, cut into large dice
- 50ml/2floz white wine
- 2 sprigs rosemary
- 4 bay leaves
- 1¼lt/5 cups lamb stock
- 3 tbsp flat leaf parsley, roughly chopped

## METHOD

- Preheat the oven to 120C/250F/Gas ½.

- Season the lamb and dust with the flour.

- Place a heavy-bottom casserole dish over a medium heat, add the olive oil and butter then the lamb.

- Fry until golden brown. Remove the lamb and keep to one side.

- Reduce the heat and fry the shallots, carrots and swede until caramelised.

- Add the wine and simmer until the liquid has reduced by half, then add the lamb back in with the lamb stock.

- Bring the stew to a simmer before adding the bay leaf and rosemary. Cover with a lid, transfer the pan to the oven and bake for one hour or until the lamb is tender.

- Add the parsley to the casserole dish and serve equally between four shallow bowls.

## CHEF'S NOTE

*The Wildlings are simple folk, who feed on food they've hunted or raided from south of The Wall. They live off the land and their wits, this is the type of meal you'd see a wildling eat around the fire.*

# Frey Pie

## Serves 8-10

## INGREDIENTS

**For the filling**

- 750g/1lb 11oz pork shoulder, minced
- 400g/14oz pork belly, finely chopped
- 250g/9oz smoked bacon, cubed
- ½ tsp ground mace
- 2 large pinches ground nutmeg
- 1 tbsp fresh chopped sage
- 1 tsp each copped thyme & pepper
- ½ tsp salt

**For the pastry**

- 550g/1¼lb plain flour
- 200g/7oz lard
- 200ml/7floz water

**To finish**

- 1 beaten egg
- 6 gelatine leaves
- 300ml/10floz chicken stock

## METHOD

Heat the oven to 180C/350F/Gas 4. In a large bowl mix together all the ingredients for the filling.

To make the pastry, put the flour in a large bowl. Add the lard and water into a small pan and heat gently until the lard is melted. Bring just to the boil and stir into the flour.

When the mixture is cool enough to handle, knead well until smooth. Cut off ¼ of the dough, wrap in cling film and reserve.Roll out the remaining dough place in the base of a non-stick 20cm springform cake tin.

Press the dough evenly over the base and up the sides of the tin. Make sure there are no holes.

Fill it with the meat and pack down well. Roll out the dough for the lid. Place on top of the pie. Pinch all around the edge to seal the pie. Make a hole for steam in the centre.

Cook in the oven for 30 mins. Reduce the heat to 150C/300F/Gas 2 and cook for another 90 mins. Brush the top with beaten egg and cook for a further 20 mins. Remove from the oven and leave until cold.

Soak the gelatine in cold water for about 5 mins. Heat the stock until almost boiling. Remove from the heat and stir in the gelatine. Leave to cool to room temperature and pour slowly through steam vent in top of pie. Leave to cool and refrigerate until firm.

### ◄ CHEF'S NOTE ►

*Winter came for House Frey when Arya took vengeance upon Lord Walder Frey for his role in the Red Wedding and the deaths of her mother and brother. Unlike the pie that Arya serves Walder Frey, this one contains no human meat, but like revenge it is a dish that's best served cold.*

# Podrick's Sensational Sausage Pot

## Serves 4

## INGREDIENTS

- 1–2 tbsp olive oil
- 12 good-quality pork sausages
- 6 rashers rindless streaky bacon, cut into 2.5cm/1in lengths
- 2 onions, thinly sliced
- 2 garlic cloves, crushed
- 1 tsp smoked paprika
- 1 tin tin chopped tomatoes
- 300ml/10floz chicken stock
- 2 tbsp tomato purée
- 1 tbsp Worcestershire sauce
- 1 tbsp dark brown muscovado sugar
- 1 tsp dried mixed herbs
- 2 bay leaves
- 3–4 sprigs fresh thyme
- 100ml/3½fl oz red or white wine
- 1 tin butter beans or mixed beans

## METHOD

- Heat a tbsp of the oil in a frying pan and cook the sausages for 10 mins until browned. Transfer to a large saucepan or a flameproof casserole dish and set aside.

- Fry the bacon pieces in the frying pan until they are crisp, then add to the sausages.

- Place the onions in the frying pan and fry for five mins until they start to soften. Add the garlic and cook for 2–3 minutes more.

- Sprinkle over the smoked paprika and cook together for a few seconds longer. Stir in the tomatoes, chicken stock, tomato purée, Worcestershire sauce, brown sugar and herbs. Pour over the wine and bring to a simmer.

- Add to the pan with the sausages and bacon. Return to a simmer, then reduce the heat, cover the pan loosely with a lid and leave to simmer very gently for 20 minutes, stirring from time to time.

- Drain the beans and rinse them in a sieve under cold running water.

- Stir the beans into the casserole, and cook for 10 minutes, stirring occasionally, until the sauce is thick and the beans are piping hot.

- Season to taste and serve with mash or fresh bread.

## ◄ CHEF'S NOTE ►

*Podrick Payne may not be one of the greatest fighters in the series, but he is quite the swordsman! After his experience in Little Finger's establishment, he became a legend - try Pod's sensational sausage for yourself.*

# Steak With Bear-naise Sauce

## Serves 4

## INGREDIENTS

- 4 steaks of your choice, cooked to your taste
- 300g/11oz butter
- 4 tbsp white wine vinegar
- 4 shallots, chopped
- 3 tbsp chopped fresh tarragon, plus 2 tbsp whole tarragon leaves
- 4 free-range egg yolks
- 1 tsp lemon juice

## METHOD

Melt the butter in a small, heavy-based saucepan over a low heat. When the butter is foaming, remove the pan from the heat and leave it to stand for a few minutes so that the white solids sink to the bottom of the pan. Sieve the butter through a fine sieve and discard the solids.

Pour the vinegar into a small pan. Add the shallots, chopped tarragon and salt, to taste.

Heat gently over a medium heat until the liquid has reduced by more than half. Strain and set aside until completely cool.

Lightly beat egg yolks with one teaspoon of water. Stir the egg yolk mixture into the cooled vinegar, then add the lemon juice.

Pour the mixture into a bowl suspended over a pan of simmering water (do not allow base of the bowl to touch the water). Whisk constantly until the sauce has thickened enough to coat the back of a spoon and has increased in volume.

Remove the bowl from the heat and slowly pour in the butter in a steady stream, whisking continuously, until the mixture is thick and smooth. Fold in the tarragon leaves and season to taste with salt and freshly ground black pepper.

Serve the sauce poured over the steaks.

## ◄ CHEF'S NOTE ►

*Bear Island is home to the ferocious Lady Lyanna Mormont. The house may not be large but it is proud and 'fights with the strength of ten mainlanders.' An army marches on its stomach and this is a meal fit for champions.*

# Bowl Of Brown

## Serves 4

## INGREDIENTS

- 2 tbsp olive oil
- 25g/1oz butter
- 750g/1lb 11oz beef stewing steak, chopped into bite-sized pieces
- 2 tbsp plain flour
- 2 garlic cloves, crushed
- 175g/6oz baby onions, peeled
- 150g/5oz celery, cut into large chunks
- 150g/5oz carrots, cut into large chunks
- 2 leeks, roughly chopped
- 200g/7oz swede, cut into large chunks
- 150ml/5floz red wine
- 500ml/2 cups beef stock
- 2 fresh bay leaves
- 3 tbsp fresh thyme leaves
- Worcestershire sauce, to taste
- 1 tbsp balsamic vinegar
- Salt and freshly ground black pepper

## METHOD

- Preheat the oven to 180C/350F/Gas 4.

- Heat the oil and butter in an ovenproof casserole dish and fry the beef until browned on all sides.

- Sprinkle over the flour and cook for a further 2-3mins.

- Add the garlic and all the vegetables and fry for 1-2mins.

- Stir in the wine, stock, herbs, Worcestershire sauce and balsamic vinegar.

- Season with salt and freshly ground black pepper.

- Cover with a lid, transfer to the oven and cook for about two hours, or until the meat is tender.

- Serve with mashed potato.

## CHEF'S NOTE

*Bowls o' brown is the common dish of Flea Bottom, the slum area of King's Landing. Brown is cooked in huge vats for years at a time and topped up with whatever ingredients happen to be available, including rats, cats or even dead bodies. This is a much more appetizing bowl of brown that the pot-shops of Flea Bottom could only have dreamed of.*

# Rabbit With Ed Sheeran

## Serves 6

### INGREDIENTS

- 2 rabbits, jointed
- 6 tbsp olive oil
- 4 garlic cloves, crushed
- 1 sprig fresh rosemary
- 2 bay leaves
- 500ml/2 cups dry white wine
- ½ lemon, juice only
- 50g/2oz seasoned flour
- 1 sliced onion
- 1 sliced celery stalk
- 8 anchovy fillets in oil
- 75g/3oz capers

## METHOD

- Place the rabbit pieces into a large bowl and add three tablespoons of the olive oil, the garlic, rosemary, bay leaves, white wine and lemon juice.

- Stir until well combined, then cover and marinate in the fridge overnight.

- Preheat the oven to 170C/325F/Gas 3.

- Remove the rabbit pieces from the marinade (but keep the marinade) and pat dry with kitchen paper. Dust the rabbit pieces in the seasoned flour and shake off any excess.

- Heat the remaining olive oil in a large pan over a medium heat.

- Add the rabbit pieces to the hot oil and fry for 4-5 minutes or until golden brown all over. Transfer to an ovenproof casserole dish.

- Pour the reserved marinade into the hot frying pan and warm through, then pour it into the casserole with the rabbit.

- Add the onion and celery to the casserole and cook in the oven for 45 minutes, or until the rabbit is tender. Add the anchovies and capers and cook for another 15 minutes.

---

### ◄ CHEF'S NOTE ►

*In a programme full of deaths, double-crossings and dragons it says a lot when perhaps the most unexpected moments of the series occurred when Ed Sheeran popped up for a campfire sing-a-long, chat and meal of roast rabbit with Arya.*

# Crown Roast

## Serves 6

## INGREDIENTS

- 1 rack of baby back ribs
- 1 tbsp olive oil
- 1 tsp salt
- ½ tsp freshly ground black pepper
- 6 cloves garlic, minced
- 1 tbsp fresh thyme, chopped
- 1½ tsp ground coriander
- 1 tbsp sherry vinegar
- ½ - 1tsp Dijon mustard
- ½ - 1tsp chopped fresh rosemary leaves

## METHOD

- Preheat the oven to 190C/375F/ Gas 5.

- Begin by bending the ribs into a semicircle (meat side in and fat side out) and using kitchen twine tie together at the base and centre, in order to hold the rack together. The rib ends should be pushed outward and look like a crown.

- Rub the pork with the olive oil. Combine the salt, pepper, garlic, thyme and coriander and press all over the meat. Place the roast in a Bundt pan with the centre of the pan coming up through the middle of the roast.

- Place on the middle rack of the oven and cook for 30 to 35mins.

- Remove from the oven, transfer the roast to a rack, cover with tin/ aluminium foil and let the meat rest for 20mins.

- While the meat is resting add the sherry vinegar, mustard and rosemary to the juices that will have gathered in the pan while cooking. Stir to combine. Taste and adjust seasoning, as needed.

- Place cooked stuffing, rice or barley in the centre of the rib crown.

- Serve the warm sauce with the roast.

## ◄ CHEF'S NOTE ►

*'When you play the Game of Thrones, you win or you die. There is no middle ground.' Cersei Lannister neatly summed up the entire series right back in episode 7. Who will sit on the Iron Throne at the end of the game remains a mystery, but for now enjoy this crown fit for a king or queen.*

# Fish From The Iron Islands

## Serves 2

### INGREDIENTS

- 2 x 175g/6oz fish fillets, like bass, haddock, snapper, cod or salmon
- Salt and ground black pepper
- 3 tbsp olive oil
- 2 tbsp butter
- 2 sprigs fresh thyme
- 1 tbsp chopped flat-leaf parsley
- Lemon wedges, to serve

## METHOD

- Pat fillets dry with a paper towel. Season on both sides with salt and pepper.

- Heat a heavy 10-inch non-stick frying pan over high heat. When the pan is hot, add the oil.

- Place the fillets in the pan, skin side down (if applicable), laying them down away from you.

- If the fillets have skin, press down gently with a spatula for about 20 seconds to prevent curling.

- Lower heat to medium and let sizzle until fish is golden and caramelized around edges, about 2-3mins.

- Carefully flip the fillets and add the butter and thyme to the pan. Tilt the pan slightly to let the melted butter pool at one end. Use a spoon to baste the fish with the butter. Continue doing this until the fish is golden all over and cooked through.

- Serve immediately with chopped parsley and lemon wedges.

### ◀ CHEF'S NOTE ▶

*The Iron Islands, home to House Greyjoy, are the rocky islands which are poor in natural resources with the exception of iron ore and the fruits of the sea which surrounds the seven islands. This recipe pays tribute to the islands greatest resources.*

# Tyrion's Leg Of Lamb

## Serves 6

## INGREDIENTS

- 1 leg of lamb
- 1 tsp of chopped rosemary
- 1 tbsp olive oil
- 2 crushed cloves of garlic

## METHOD

- Rub all of the ingredients over the lamb and leave to marinate for at least an hour or preferably overnight.

- Preheat the oven to 220C/425F/Gas 7.

- Cook the lamb in a roasting tin for around 1½hrs. (A 3kg joint would take around 1hr 30mins for medium cooked lamb. A larger piece of meat will take longer)

- The outside should be crispy and the meat inside slightly pink.

- Serve thinly sliced as the heart of a mealtime feast.

## CHEF'S NOTE

*When Tyrion Lannister is imprisoned and starving, a dish of roast lamb with peas and onions, fresh bread and butter and a flagon of wine is what he most desires and cheekily asks for. Alas all he is given is beans. Thankfully, we can still enjoy the food of Tyrion's dreams.*

# Honeyed Chicken

## Serves 2

## INGREDIENTS

- 2 large chicken breasts
- Half a lemon
- 1 tbsp honey
- 1 tbsp dark soy sauce

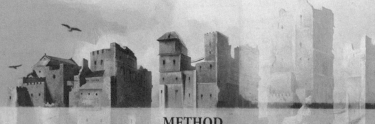

## METHOD

- Preheat the oven to 190C/375F/Gas 5

- Put the chicken breasts, skin side up in a small baking dish and season.

- Squeeze the lemon into a bowl along with the honey and soy sauce.

- Spoon the mixture over the chicken, then tuck the squeezed-out half of lemon between the pieces .

- Roast the chicken breasts in a baking dish, uncovered, for 30-35mins or until cooked through and richly glazed, basting with the juices at least twice.

## ◄ CHEF'S NOTE ►

*This recipe takes us right back to the beginning of the series when the Stark family were all still alive and living at Winterfell. After discovering a pack of direwolves with a dead mother, Jon Snow convinces Ned Stark to allow the children to keep one each. This is the meal that Jon shares with his 'runt of the litter' wolf - Ghost.*

# Arya's Oysters & Cockles Linguine

## Serves 2

## INGREDIENTS

- 225g/8oz uncooked linguine
- 1 tbsp olive oil
- 2 crushed large garlic cloves
- A big pinch crushed red chili flakes
- 300ml/10 ½ floz fish stock
- ¼ tsp ground black pepper
- 1 tin of medium smoked oysters, drained
- 1 jar of pickled cockles, drained & rinsed
- A large handful chopped fresh parsley

## METHOD

Cook the pasta according to package instructions. Drain it, reserving a cup of the pasta cooking water.

Whilst the pasta is cooking heat the olive oil in a large pan with deep sides.

Add the garlic and crushed red chili flakes and cook for 30 seconds, stirring constantly.

Pour in the fish stock and the pasta cooking water. Bring to a boil, then reduce heat and let simmer until reduced and thickened slightly - this will take around 5mins.

Add the drained oysters and cockles and stir until the sauce comes together and the liquid just comes back to a simmer.

Add the drained pasta and parsley, then toss until evenly coated. Let it cook for another minute.

Taste and add more pepper, crushed chilli or salt to your liking.

## ◄ CHEF'S NOTE ►

*When Arya is in training at the House of Black and White, in order to become 'no one' and carry out her assassin tasks, she must learn to become an invisible face in the crowd. When stalking her intended victim she becomes Lana an orphan child wandering the street of Braavos, selling oysters and cockles.*

# Daenerys' Heart

## Serves 4

## INGREDIENTS

**For the stuffing**

- 1 tbsp butter
- 1 small onion, finely chopped
- 1 crushed clove of garlic
- 50g/2oz mushrooms, finely diced
- 75g/3oz good quality sausage meat
- 1 tbsp fresh parsley, finely chopped
- 1 beaten egg

**For the sauce**

- 25g/1oz butter
- 1 each tbsp plain flour & butter
- 175ml/6floz hot lamb, or beef stock
- 1 tin of chopped tomatoes
- 75ml/2½fl oz red wine
- 4 prepared lambs hearts (tubes removed and trimmed of excess fat)
- 8 rashers smoked streaky bacon
- 2 tbsp finely chopped parsley

## METHOD

- Preheat the oven to 180C/350F/Gas 4.

- Make the stuffing by melting the butter in a frying pan, add the onion and cook over a medium heat for 2-3mins, add the mushrooms and continue to cook for 2 mins. Allow the mixture to cool.

- Combined the cooled mixture with the sausage meat, parsley, seasoning and egg and mix well.

- Make the sauce by heating the butter in the frying pan, add the flour and cook for 1-2mins.

- Add the stock, tomatoes & wine, bring to the boil, reduce the heat and simmer for 5 mins.

- Spoon the stuffing into the prepared hearts. Wrap the hearts with 2 rashers of bacon and tie with string.

- Heat the other tbsp of butter in the pan and brown the hearts on both sides and transfer to an ovenproof dish.

- Pour the sauce over the hearts and cook in the preheated oven for about two hours or until tender.

- Remove the string, slice and return to the sauce, stir through the chopped parsley and serve.

### ◄ CHEF'S NOTE ►

*Daenerys Targaryen becomes the Khaleesi after performing a Dothraki ceremony when pregnant with the Khal's child. By consuming a raw stallion's heart Daenerys proves herself to the group and demonstrates that her unborn child will be strong. Unfortunately, it seems eating hearts didn't guarantee her infant's health.*

# Pigeon Pie

## Serves 2

## INGREDIENTS

- 1 woodpigeon
- 2 shallots, halved
- 1 stick celery, roughly chopped
- 2 sprigs rosemary
- 2 sprigs thyme
- 1 bay leaf
- 300ml/10½floz medium dry cider
- 1 medium onion, peeled & finely chopped
- 1 carrot, peeled & diced
- 1 parsnip, peeled & diced
- 1 sprig thyme, leaves picked
- 2 discs ready rolled puff pastry, large enough to cover the top of your pie dish
- 1 beaten egg

## METHOD

- Preheat the oven to 170°C/ 325F/Gas 3.

- Place the woodpigeon in a small roasting pan, breast side down. Arrange the onion, celery and herbs around it and pour in the cider. Cover with tin foil and cook for 1 hour. Turn the pigeon so it is breast side up and braise for a further 20 minutes.

- Once cooled, remove all the meat from the bones and strain the liquid through a fine sieve into a bowl. Set aside.

- Increase oven temperature to 180C/ 350F/ Gas 4.

- Fry the onion and celery on a medium heat for 2-3 mins before adding the carrot, parsnip and thyme

- Sauté until soft, then add the cooking liquid to the pan. Reduce slightly then add the pigeon. Stir to combine and remove from the heat.

- Spoon into 2 individual pie dishes, top with the pastry, brush with the beaten egg and bake for 15 minutes, or until the pastry is golden brown.

## ◄ CHEF'S NOTE ►

*Pigeon pie is the traditional meal served at wedding feasts. During the purple wedding of Joffrey Baratheon to Margaery Tyrell a pie is served so large that it contains a whole flock of live pigeons which fly out as Joffrey tests out his new sword christened Widow's Wail.*

# DRAGON DESSERTS

# Red Wedding Cake

### Serves 8

## INGREDIENTS

**For the red velvet cake**
- 150g/5oz unsalted butter, softened
- 150g/5oz golden caster sugar
- 1 tsp vanilla extract
- 3 free-range eggs, lightly beaten
- 4 tbsp Greek-style yoghurt
- 1-2 drops red food colouring gel
- 150g/5oz self-raising flour
- 50g/2oz cocoa powder
- 1 tbsp semi-skimmed milk

**For the icing**
- 100g/3½oz butter
- 200g/7oz cream cheese
- 500g/1lb 2oz icing sugar
- 1 tsp lemon juice

## METHOD

- Pre heat the oven to 170C/325F/gas 3. Grease and line a deep, round 15cm/ 6in tin.

- Beat the butter, sugar and vanilla together in a bowl until pale and fluffy. Add the eggs one at a time, beating after each addition (if the mixture looks curdled add a spoonful of the flour).

- Mix the yogurt with the food colouring and beat the yogurt into the cake mixture.

- Fold in the remaining flour and cocoa powder, followed by the milk until well combined. Spoon the mixture into the cake tin and bake for 1 hour 20 minutes or until well risen and a skewer comes out clean.

- Remove the cake from the tin and leave to cool for five minutes, then place onto a cooling rack and set aside to cool completely.

- For the icing, mix the butter and cream cheese together in a bowl. Then beat in the icing sugar a little at a time. Once all the icing sugar has been added, add the lemon juice and beat the icing for five minutes or until pale in colour.

- Slice the cake into three equal layers and sandwich them together with the icing. Finish with a layer of icing on top.

### ◄ CHEF'S NOTE ►

*Maybe the events of the Red Wedding would have been less bloody if the Stark's and the Frey's had sat down with a big slice of red velvet cake instead. Rob and Catelyn may be no more but we can still enjoy one of the best and most shocking episodes (just make sure the knife is only used to cut the cake!)*

# Sansa's Lemon Cakes

## Serves 12

## INGREDIENTS

- Nonstick vegetable oil spray
- 500g/1lb 2oz plain flour
- 2 tsp baking powder
- ¾ tsp salt
- ¼ tsp baking soda
- 120ml/½ cup buttermilk
- 2 tbsp finely grated lemon zest
- 1tsp vanilla extract
- 120ml/4floz fresh lemon juice
- 125g/4oz soft unsalted butter
- 400g/7oz sugar, divided
- 3 large eggs
- 1 lemon, thinly sliced

## METHOD

- Preheat oven to 175°C/350°F/Gas4. Coat an 8x8" pan with non-stick spray. Line the bottom of pan with grease proof paper.

- Sift the flour, baking powder, salt & baking soda in a medium bowl. Combine the buttermilk, lemon zest, vanilla, and half of the lemon juice in a large measuring cup.

- Using an electric mixer on medium-high speed, beat the butter and 250g sugar in a large bowl until light and fluffy. Add the eggs one at a time then continue to beat until it is almost doubled in volume, very light, airy, and pale yellow.

- Reduce mixer speed and add the dry ingredients alternating with buttermilk.

- Scrape batter into the prepared pan and smooth the top. Bake until just light golden and a skewer inserted into the centre comes out clean, this should take 25–30 minutes. Transfer pan to a wire rack; let cool for at least 1 hour.

- Meanwhile, bring the remaining sugar and 3tbsp water to a boil in a small saucepan, stirring occasionally, until the sugar is dissolved. Add the lemon slices to the boiling syrup. Turn off heat and let cool for 1 hour. Stir in remaining lemon juice.

- Transfer cooled cake to a work surface. Cut into 12 cakes. Drizzle each with lemon syrup and top with lemon slices.

## ◄ CHEF'S NOTE ►

*'Lemon cakes are my favourite' proclaims Sansa and she bonds with Olenna Tyrell whilst eating them. Sansa is the character who has arguably grown the most over the series and like her these cakes are complex- sweet and sour at the same time. A dessert suitable for the Lady of Winterfell.*

# Ice & Fire

## Serves 4

### INGREDIENTS

- 8 scoops vanilla ice cream
- 300g/11oz dark chocolate
- Pinch chilli flakes
- 200ml/7floz whole milk
- 100ml/3½floz double cream
- 25g/1oz golden caster sugar

### METHOD

- Put the chocolate and chilli in a large bowl. Bring the milk, cream and sugar to the boil, then remove from heat and pour over the chocolate.

- Leave to stand for 2 mins, then whisk until the chocolate is melted.

- Serve warm with scoops of ice cream.

### ◄ CHEF'S NOTE ►

*Fire and ice is at the heart of Game of Thrones. In fact the whole series of books- A Song of Ice and Fire is named after them. The contrast and combination between the two is central to the themes and look of the series and to this dessert too. The icy chill of the creamy ice cream contrasting with the fiery warmth of the chocolate chilli sauce is a sensory overload.*

# Mother Of Dragon Fruit

## Serves 8

## INGREDIENTS

- 75g/3oz butter, melted and cooled, plus extra for greasing
- 275g/10oz shop-bought filo pastry
- 4 tbsp apricot jam
- 500g/1lb 2oz Greek yoghurt
- 2 tbsp honey
- 1 vanilla pod, seeds only (or 2 drops of vanilla extract)
- Small bunch black seedless grapes, halved
- Bunch of redcurrants
- 1 dragon fruit, peeled and cubed
- 2 large figs, quartered

## METHOD

- Preheat the oven to 180C/350F/Gas 4. Grease a 12-hole muffin tin or cupcake tin well.

- Cut the filo pastry into squares that are big enough to fit into the muffin holes and hang over the sides a little. Brush each piece of filo with lots of melted butter to stop it from burning in the oven, then push a filo square into eight of the holes and top with another filo square, you will need to layer up 3–4 pieces

- Place the filo cases into the oven for five minutes. Once they are golden-brown and crispy, remove them from the oven and leave to cool for 10 minutes. Remove them from the muffin tray and place them on serving dishes.

- Mix the Greek yoghurt, honey and vanilla together in a bowl and then place a good dollop into each pastry case. Divide the fruit among the tartlets, piling it up high. Brush with the warm apricot jam to make a shiny glaze and serve.

## CHEF'S NOTE

*Dany has more titles than she's had hot dinners - Daenerys of the House Targaryen, the First of Her Name, The Unburnt, Queen of the Andals, the Rhoynar and the First Men, Queen of Meereen, Khaleesi of the Great Grass Sea, Protector of the Realm, Lady Regnant of the Seven Kingdoms, Breaker of Chains. But the one everyone remembers is - Mother of Dragons. The fruits in this dessert come from the lands that Daenerys has travelled whilst she's built her army.*

# Queen Of Puddings

## Serves 6

## INGREDIENTS

**For the base**

- \ 600ml/1pt full-fat milk
- \ 25g/1oz butter, plus extra for greasing the dish
- \ 1 lemon, zest finely grated
- \ 50g/2oz caster sugar
- \ 3 free-range eggs, yolks only
- \ 75g/3oz fresh white breadcrumbs

**For the meringue**

- \ 175g/6oz caster sugar
- \ 3 free-range eggs, whites only
- \ 5tbsp raspberry jam

## METHOD

\ Preheat the oven to 170C/325F/Gas 3 and grease a large ovenproof dish with butter.

\ For the base, very gently warm the milk in a small saucepan. Add the butter, lemon zest and 50g of sugar, stir until dissolved.

\ Make a custard by lightly whisking the egg yolks in a bowl. Slowly pour the warm milk into the eggs, while still whisking. Place breadcrumbs in the base of the buttered dish and add the custard. Leave for 15 mins so the crumbs absorb the liquid.

\ Transfer the dish to a roasting tin and fill the tin halfway with hot water. Bake in the oven for about 25 mins or until it has set. Remove from the oven and set aside to cool a little.

\ Whisk the egg whites until stiff peaks form. Add the remaining 175g/6oz sugar a teaspoon at a time, still whisking on maximum speed until the mixture is stiff and shiny. Transfer the meringue mixture to a piping bag.

\ Spread the jam over the set custard, then pipe the meringue on top.

\ Lower the oven temperature to 150C/300F/Gas 2 and return the pudding to the oven (not in the roasting tin with water) for about 25-30 minutes until the meringue is pale golden all over and crisp. Serve at once with pouring cream.

## ◄ CHEF'S NOTE ►

*There are many Queens in Game of Thrones, some official like Cersei Lannister or Margaery Tyrell and some self-declared like Selyse Baratheon or Yara Greyjoy. There's enough of this pudding to go round and for every Queen to have a feast.*

# The House Of Black & White Cheesecake

## Serves 8

### INGREDIENTS

- 300g/11oz Oreo cookies
- 50g/2oz melted butter
- 600g/1lb 5oz cream cheese
- 2 tbsp plain flour
- 100g/3½oz golden caster sugar
- Vanilla extract
- 2 eggs + 1 yolk
- 300ml/10½floz sour cream
- 200g /7oz white chocolate, melted and cooled a little

## METHOD

- Preheat the oven to 180C/350F/Gas 4. Pull apart the biscuits and scrape out the filling (discard or eat!). Blend the biscuits until you have only crumbs, pour in the butter then mix.

- Press into the base of a 20cm springform tin and bake for 5 minutes, then leave to cool.

- Beat the soft cheese with the flour, sugar, a few drops of vanilla, eggs, the yolk and about half of the sour cream until light and fluffy.

- Stir in the white chocolate and pour into the tin. Bake for 40 minutes and then check – it should be set, but wobbly in the centre.

- Leave in the tin to cool completely (if you can, leave it in the oven to cool with the door open a little, it shouldn't crack).

- Spread the rest of the sour cream over the surface then chill for 2-3 hours or preferably overnight.

### ⊸ CHEF'S NOTE ⊷

*Named after the temple in Braavos, dedicated to the Many Faced God and headquarters of the mysterious assassins, the Faceless Men. It is here that Arya trains to become 'no one' and encounters the Hall of Faces. This cheesecake reflects the black and white with white chocolate cheesecake on a black cookie base.*

# Game Of Scones

Serves 10

## INGREDIENTS

- 225g/8oz self-raising flour
- Pinch of salt
- 55g/2oz butter
- 25g/1oz caster sugar
- 150ml/5floz milk
- 1 free-range egg, beaten, to glaze

## METHOD

- Heat the oven to 220C/425F/Gas 7. Lightly grease a baking sheet.

- Mix together the flour and salt and use your thumbs to rub in the butter.

- Stir in the sugar and then the milk to form a soft dough.

- Turn on to a floured work surface and knead very lightly. Pat out to around 2cm/¾in thick. Use a 5cm/2in cutter to stamp out rounds and place on a baking sheet.

- Lightly knead together the rest of the dough and stamp out more scones to use it all up.

- Brush the tops of the scones with the beaten egg. Bake for 12-15 minutes or until well risen and golden

- Cool on a wire rack and serve with clotted cream and good jam.

### ◄ CHEF'S NOTE ►

*Game of Thrones is the book where the series all began. The power struggles, the passion, the feuds, the battles, the dragons, the wights and the magic. All began when A Game of Thrones was published back in 1996. George R. R. Martin may be taking his time in finishing the series but we have the epic visuals of the television show (and Kit Harington) to keep us entertained in the meantime.*

# Bran Brownies

## Serves 12

### INGREDIENTS

- 250g/9oz All-Bran cereal
- 150ml/5floz boiling water
- 150g/5oz of plain flour
- 75g/3oz cocoa
- ¼ tsp salt
- 4 eggs
- 125ml/½ cup of flavourless oil
- 400g/14oz granulated sugar
- 1 tsp vanilla extract
- 150g/5oz chocolate chips

## METHOD

- Preheat the oven to 180°C/ 350°F/ Gas 4.

- Grease a 33 x 23 cm (13 x 9-inch) baking pan with non-stick cooking spray.

- In large bowl, stir together the cereal and boiling water. Leave to stand for 5 minutes or until the bran has softened.

- In a medium bowl, sift together the flour, cocoa and salt.

- Stir the eggs, oil, sugar and vanilla into the softened cereal and mix well.

- Stir in the flour mixture until well combined. Stir in the chocolate chips.

- Spread the mix in the prepared tin and bake for 20 mins or until centre 'gives' slightly when touched with a finger. Leave to cool completely before cutting into 12 brownies.

## ◄ CHEF'S NOTE ►

*Brandon, or Bran, is the fourth child of Ned and Catelyn Stark. We were first introduced to him as an adventurous boy who loved climbing but when he saw something he shouldn't, Jaime Lannister had to make sure he couldn't spill the secret of the twins. It didn't work out quite as planned but Bran in his new role as the Three-Eyed Raven may have the best tools needed to defeat the Night King.*

# Iced Little Fingers

## Serves 12

## INGREDIENTS

**For the dough**
- 500g/1lb 2oz strong white flour
- 50g/2oz caster sugar
- 40g/1½oz unsalted butter, softened
- 2 free-range eggs
- 2 x 7g/¼oz sachets instant yeast
- 2 tsp salt
- 150ml/5floz warm milk
- 120ml/4floz water

**For the icing**
- 200g/7oz icing sugar
- 5 tsp cold water
- For the filling
- 200ml/7floz whipping cream
- 125g/4oz strawberry jam
- Icing sugar, for dusting

## METHOD

- Preheat the oven to 220C/425F/Gas 7.

- Place all of the ingredients into a large bowl. Combine with your hands to form a dough.

- Turn the dough onto a lightly floured surface and knead well for 15 minutes. Return the dough to the bowl, cover with a damp cloth and leave to rise for one hour.

- Divide the dough into 12 pieces, then roll into balls and shape into fingers 5in long.

- Place the dough fingers onto a greased baking tray, leaving space for them to double in size and set aside in a warm place for 40 minutes. Bake in the oven for 10 minutes then set them aside to cool.

- For the icing, sift the icing sugar in a wide bowl and gradually stir in the cold water to form a thick paste

- Dip the top of the cooled fingers into the icing, smoothing it with the back of a spoon then leave to set on a wire rack.

- Lightly whip the cream and spoon it into a piping bag fitted with a small nozzle. Spoon the strawberry jam into another piping bag.

- Slice the iced fingers horizontally, leaving one long edge intact. Pipe in a generous line of whipped cream into the middle of each finger, then a thinner line of jam. Dust the iced fingers with icing sugar and serve.

## ◄ CHEF'S NOTE ►

*Petyr Baelish is one of the most manipulative characters in Game of Thrones. Lord Baelish wears many hats. Called Littlefinger as his father was lord of the smallest of the Finger Isles; he hates the name as he sees it as belittling. Unlike Petyr Baelish, these iced fingers are sweet, lovely and you will want to spend time in their company.*

# Sweetgrass & Strawberries

## Serves 4

## INGREDIENTS

- 4 handfuls strawberries
- 1 tbsp caster sugar
- 1 vanilla pod, scored lengthways and seeds scraped out
- 1 splash balsamic vinegar
- 1 pot crème fraîche
- A few small fresh mint leaves
- Zest of 1 orange

## METHOD

- Put the strawberries in a bowl and add the sugar, half the vanilla seeds and the vinegar.

- Squash together with the back of a fork and leave to macerate for 10–15 minutes.

- Stir the rest of the vanilla seeds into the crème fraiche.

- To serve, spoon a little vanilla cream in the centre of each bowl, make a well in the middle and spoon in some mushed strawberries.

- Scatter over the mint leaves and orange zest then serve.

## CHEF'S NOTE

*At The Hand's Tourney Feast, 'tables and benches had been raised outside the pavilions, piled high with sweetgrass and strawberries and fresh-baked bread' are feasted upon by Sansa back when she still dreamed of marrying Joffrey. Recreate the hedonistic summer and feel part of a royal feast by dining on these succulent strawberries.*

# Honeycake

## Serves 8

## INGREDIENTS

**For the cake**
- 175g/6oz clear honey
- 150g/5oz butter
- 75g/3oz light muscovado sugar
- 2 beaten eggs
- 200g/7oz sifted self-raising flour

**For the icing**
- 50g/2oz icing sugar
- 1 tbsp clear honey

## METHOD

- Preheat the oven to 180C/350F/Gas 4 and butter and line the bottom of a 7in/18cm cake tin.

- Measure the honey, butter and sugar into a large pan. Add a tablespoon of water and heat gently until melted.

- Remove from the heat and mix in the eggs and flour.

- Spoon into the cake tin and bake for 40-45 minutes until the cake is springy to the touch and shrinking slightly from the sides of the tin.

- Cool slightly in the tin before turning out onto a wire cooling rack.

- While the cake is still warm, make the icing by mixing the sugar and honey together with 2-3tsps of hot water. Drizzle the icing over the cake.

## ◄ CHEF'S NOTE ►

*Another cake beloved by Sansa Stark 'she still remembers the innkeep, a fat woman named Masha Heddle who chewed sourleaf night and day and seemed to have an endless supply of smiles and sweet cakes for the children. The sweet cakes had been soaked with honey, rich and heavy on the tongue...' This honeycake is just as memorable.*

# Castle Black Forest Parfait

### Serves 6

## INGREDIENTS

- 600ml/1pt double cream
- ½ tsp vanilla extract
- 2 tbsp icing sugar
- 250g/9oz chocolate cake
- 400g/14oz black cherries in kirsch, drained, reserving the liquid for drizzling
- 50g/2oz chopped dark chocolate

## METHOD

- Whisk the cream with the vanilla and icing sugar until it just holds its shape.

- Crumble the cake into six glasses, then top with a few cherries, a dollop of cream and a drizzle of the kirsch.

- Sprinkle the chopped chocolate over the top.

### CHEF'S NOTE

*Castle Black is the primary headquarters of the Night's Watch. The Watch is divided into three orders; The Rangers- who are the man fighting force, The Builders- who maintain The Wall, and The Stewards who gather and cook for The Watch. Life is simple and frugal at The Wall and it's a pretty safe bet the Stewards never made anything this tasty – but that's no reason we can't indulge.*

# Valyrian Steel Cut Oatmeal Biscuits

## Serves 20

### INGREDIENTS

- 50g/2oz steel cut oats
- 75g/3oz wholemeal flour, plus a little extra for dusting
- Pinch fine sea salt
- ½ tsp bicarbonate of soda
- ½ tsp ground mixed spice
- 75g/3oz butter, plus extra for greasing
- 50g/2oz apple sauce

### METHOD

- Preheat the oven to 190C/375F/Gas 5 and grease and flour two baking sheets.

- Mix together the oats, flour, salt, bicarbonate of soda and mixed spice.

- Cream the butter in a bowl and beat in the apple sauce, a little at a time. Beat in the oat mixture

- Place walnut sized portions of the mixture on a baking sheet, leaving a space of about 5cm/2in round each one. Flatten them slightly, with a fork.

- Bake the biscuits for 15 minutes or until they are beginning to turn golden.

- Leave the biscuits on the baking trays until they are cool and firm.

### ◄ CHEF'S NOTE ►

*Valyrian steel is the ancient metal forged in the days of the Valyrian Freehold. Famed for its light weight, strength and ability to remain sharp forever without ever needing to be sharpened. Although not many realise it, it is one of the few substances that can kill White Walkers. These biscuits aren't sweet but rather are best served with cheese and grapes to finish a Game of Thrones feast.*

# Highgarden Rose Meringues

## Serves 20

## INGREDIENTS

**For the meringues**
- 3 medium free-range egg whites
- 125g/4oz caster sugar
- 50g/2oz icing sugar
- 1 tsp rosewater
- Couple of drops of red or pink food colouring

**For the fillings**
- 2 tbsp double cream
- 50g/2oz white chocolate, broken into pieces
- 25g/1oz raspberries, finely chopped
- 150ml/5floz whipped cream

## METHOD

- To make the meringues, preheat the oven to it's lowest setting. Line 2 baking trays with baking paper.

- Whisk the egg whites in a clean glass bowl until soft peaks form.

- Whisk in the sugar a tablespoon at a time until the mixture is thick, smooth and glossy. Sift over the icing sugar then fold in. Fold in the rosewater and food colouring.

- Place the mixture in tsp sizes onto the pre-pared baking trays to make about 40 small meringues. Bake for 2 hours then remove from the oven and leave to cool.

- To make the raspberry filling, heat the cream in a small saucepan until just boiling.

- Remove from the heat and stir in the white chocolate. Mix in the raspberries. Leave to cool a little.

- Make the mini meringues by using a teaspoon of raspberry filling to sandwich together 2 meringues.

## ◄ CHEF'S NOTE ►

*Highgarden was the seat of House Tyrell and the capital of The Reach. Highgarden sits on the Roseroad, a thoroughfare linking King's landing and Oldtown. It is surrounded by golden roses and green fields and it is these which inspire the Tyrell sigel. The perfumed depth of the rosewater in these meringues will let you dream you're back at Highgarden in its glory days.*

# Varys' Lavender Panna Cotta

## Serves 6

## INGREDIENTS

**For the lavender flowers**
- 225ml/8floz water
- 100g/3½oz caster sugar
- A handful of lavender flowers

**For the panna cotta**
- 600ml/1 pint 1½floz double cream
- 50g/2oz vanilla sugar
- Zest of 1 orange
- 2 tsp gelatine

## METHOD

- First begin by making the lavender flowers. Heat the water and caster sugar together in a pan, stir until the sugar melts and then boil steadily, so that the liquid can reduce a little.

- Take the pan off the heat and leave to cool.

- When the sugar has cooled, add the lavender flowers to the pan.

- For the panna cotta, line six ramekins with cling film and place on a tray. Warm three quarters of the cream with the vanilla sugar and orange zest in a pan, taking care not to allow the cream to boil.

- Strain the mixture through a sieve into a mixing bowl.

- Sprinkle 2 tbsp of water over the gelatine until it becomes spongy. Heat very gently in a clean pan over a low heat until it dissolves.

- Add the cream mixture to the gelatine and take off the heat. Leave to cool.

- Softly whip the remaining cream and add the cream to the gelatine mixture.

- Pour the mixture into the lined ramekins and transfer to the fridge to chill for at least 2 hours.

- Turn the panna cotta out onto individual serving plates and drizzle the lavender syrup over them. Decorate with the sugary lavender flowers.

## ◄ CHEF'S NOTE ►

*Varys or The Spider is something of an enigma. As cunning as Little Finger he however appears to lack the personal ambition. Made a eunuch at a young age he is soft, bald and fat. He takes pride in his appearance and is described as smelling of lilacs, rosewater and lavender. If this dessert was in human form, it would be Varys shaped.*

# King's Layer Cake

## Serves 8

## INGREDIENTS

**For the cake**
- 3 eggs, separated
- 3 tbsp of hot water
- 75g/3oz caster sugar
- 50g/2oz plain flour
- 50g/2oz cornflour
- 1 tsp of baking powder
- Icing sugar to dust

**For the Filling**
- 450g/1lb full fat Greek yogurt
- 1 vanilla pod, split and seeds removed
- 450g/1lb fresh raspberries
- 120ml/4floz sweet white wine

## METHOD

- Preheat oven to 180°C/350°F/Gas 4. Grease a 25cm (10 inch) high-sided cake tin with a little vegetable oil and then dust with caster sugar.

- To make the sponge, whisk together the egg yolks and hot water until foamy using an electric whisk. Slowly add two thirds of the sugar and continue whisking on a high speed until thick and creamy.

- In a clean bowl whisk the egg whites until stiff, slowly adding the remaining sugar 1 dessert spoon at a time, allowing 10 seconds between each addition. Carefully fold the egg whites into the yolk mixture

- Sift the flour, cornflour and baking powder over and carefully fold into the mixture.

- Pour into the prepared tin and bake in the centre of a preheated oven for 20-25 minutes, until firm to the touch. Allow to cool.

- When cool, cut the cake horizontally into three sections. Add the vanilla seeds to the yogurt and mix well.

- Place the base sponge on a serving plate, drizzle with a third of the wine, spread with half of the yogurt then add half of the raspberries. Top with the centre sponge repeating the process. Top with the remaining sponge, drizzle with wine and dust with icing sugar.

## ◄ CHEF'S NOTE ►

*Layered would be the perfect description for Jaime Lannister, from the incestuous hand who literally stabbed his king in the back to one of the few remaining characters with a moral center remaining. The golden sponge in this cake represents the golden Lannister hair he's famed for and the raspberry red of the Lannister banners.*

# KINGSLAYER
# COCKTAILS

# Winter Is Coming

## Serves 12

### INGREDIENTS

- 2 x 75cl bottles medium to full-bodied red wine
- 1 orange stuck with cloves
- 2 oranges, sliced
- 2 lemons, sliced
- 6 level tbsp brown sugar
- 1 cinnamon stick
- 2 level tsp finely grated fresh ginger
- 2 tbsp fruit liqueur such as Cointreau, Grand Marnier or cherry brandy (optional)

## METHOD

- Put all the ingredients in a saucepan with 2½ pints (1.5 litres) water then heat to simmering point, stirring until all the sugar has dissolved.

- Keep it barely at simmering point for at least 20 minutes (but do not boil or all the alcohol will evaporate).

- If having a party this can be made in advance, then re-heated just before serving.

### ◄ CHEF'S NOTE ►

*Cersei Lannister is a woman of many loves; her children, her brother/ lover Jaime, money, power but perhaps, based on how often she's seen lovingly caressing a glass, red wine would be her greatest love of all. Winter is coming and this spiced, mulled version will warm even the coldest of hearts.*

# Stark & Stormy

## Serves 1

## INGREDIENTS

- 50ml/2floz dark rum
- 25ml/1floz fresh lime juice, plus a wedge to serve
- 100ml/3½floz chilled ginger beer (a good fiery variety)
- Lime wedge to garnish

## METHOD

- Put all the ingredients in a Collins or Highball glass over lots of ice.

- Stir gently and garnish with a wedge of lime.

## ◄ CHEF'S NOTE ►

*The stark family is smaller than it was at the beginning of the series but those that remain standing have a fiery kick and pack a punch, much like this cocktail. The heat and warmth of the ginger beer and rum work perfectly with the tangy lime. A few of these would help you prepare for the war that is coming.*

# The Imp

## Serves 1

## INGREDIENTS

- 50ml/2oz bourbon
- 1 tbsp fresh lemon juice
- 2 tbsp simple syrup (1 part water, 1 part sugar)
- A cherry to garnish
- A lemon wedge to garnish

## METHOD

- Add all the ingredients to a shaker filled with ice and shake.

- Strain into a rocks/ old fashioned glass filled with fresh ice.

- Garnish with a cherry and lemon wedge.

### CHEF'S NOTE

*'That's what I do: I drink and I know things.' Much like his sister, Tyrion Lannister is no stranger to alcohol. Like him, this drink is strong, with a great mix of sweet and sour. In keeping with its namesake, it's naturally a short.*

# Beyond The Wall

### Serves 2

## INGREDIENTS

- 250ml/8½floz Cointreau or triple sec
- 120ml/4floz lemon juice
- 250ml/8½floz tequila
- 2 handfuls of ice
- Lime slices, to garnish

## METHOD

- Place the Cointreau (or triple sec), lemon juice, tequila and ice in a blender.

- Blend, pour into glasses, add a lime slice, and serve with a straw.

## CHEF'S NOTE

*North of The Wall is the area of Westeros inhabited by the White Walkers. Bleak, cold and desolate the far north is a wild land so scary they had to build a wall over 700ft tall to defend the realm from the wildlings that inhabit it. Maybe the Night King would be less serious if he'd had a few of these!*

# Wildfire

## Serves 1

### INGREDIENTS

- 75ml/2½floz cognac
- 5ml/1tsp absinthe
- Lemon twist to garnish
- 2 handfulsof ice cubes

## METHOD

- Stir cognac and absinthe in a cocktail shaker filled with ice.

- Strain into a chilled cocktail glass and garnish with a lemon twist.

### CHEF'S NOTE

*Wildfire is a lethal green flammable liquid with becomes more potent as it ages and has long associations with madness - much like the absinthe in this cocktail!*

# The Red Priestess

## Serves 1

## INGREDIENTS

- 50ml/2floz vodka
- 120ml/4floz cranberry juice
- 25ml/1floz orange juice

## METHOD

- Fill a tall glass with ice.

- Pour in the vodka and fill the glass to three quarters full with cranberry juice.

- Top with orange juice.

- Stir and serve.

### ◄ CHEF'S NOTE ►

*Melisandre unwaveringly worships the Lord of Light, leading her to manipulate others into deadly and cruel actions that will seemingly please him. Born a slave in Essos, Melisandre is a member of the clergy in the faith of R'hllor and her red robes, hair and ruby necklace show the importance of the colour. Take inspiration in this scarlet sensation.*

# Needle

## Serves 1

## INGREDIENTS

- Juice of 1 lime
- 1 tsp granulated sugar leaves
- Small handful mint plus extra sprig to serve
- 60ml/2floz white rum
- Soda water, to taste

## METHOD

- Muddle the lime juice, sugar and mint leaves in a small jug or cup, crushing the mint as you go – you can use the end of a rolling pin for this.

- Pour into a tall glass and add a handful of ice.

- Pour over the rum, stirring with a long handled spoon.

- Top up with soda water, garnish with mint and serve.

## ◄ CHEF'S NOTE ►

*Sharp, strong and powerful, this is a drink that is inspired by Arya Stark's sword, a gift from Jon Snow. It also pays homage to the water dance style of fencing that she's perfected and uses in her quest to cross off her list of those who have wronged her and her family.*

# Blood Of Dragons

## Serves 1

### INGREDIENTS

- 1 lemon wedge
- 1 lime wedge
- 60ml/2oz vodka
- 120ml/4oz tomato juice
- 2 dashes Tabasco sauce
- 2 dashes Worcestershire sauce
- 1 pinch celery salt
- 1 pinch ground black pepper
- 1 pinch smoked paprika

## METHOD

- Pour some celery salt onto a small plate and rub the cut of the lemon or lime wedge along the rim of a highball glass.

- Roll the outer edge of the glass in celery salt until fully coated.

- Squeeze the lemon and lime wedges into a shaker and drop them in alongside the remaining ingredients and ice and shake.

- Strain into the prepared glass.

### ◄ CHEF'S NOTE ►

*Dragons are one of the most remarkable things about the lands of fire and ice. Long believed to be extinct, Daenerys Targaryen; The Mother of Dragons has brought them back life. Pay homage to the fearsome beasts with the hot and fiery Bloody Mary.*

# Joffrey's Cupbearer

### Serves 1

## INGREDIENTS

- 1 sugar cube
- 3 dashes of angostura bitters
- 150ml/5floz chilled Champagne or sparkling wine
- 1 lemon twist, for garnish

## METHOD

- In a champagne flute soak the sugar cube with the Angostura bitters.

- Add the Champagne.

- Garnish the drink with the lemon twist.

## ◄ CHEF'S NOTE ►

*King Joffrey's death at the Purple Wedding led many to breathe a sigh of relief that the tyrants bloody and sadistic reign was over. His uncle Tyrion may have been arrested for the crime but the true poisoner was left a mystery for quite some time, until she revealed the truth in the coldest and classiest way possible. Raise a glass to the baddest matriarch in the Seven Kingdoms - Olenna Tyrell.*

# Forbidden Fire & Ice

## Serves 1

### INGREDIENTS

- 50ml/2floz gin
- 200ml/7floz tomato juice
- ½ bottle ale
- Tabasco sauce (to taste)
- Ice cubes (crushed)

## METHOD

- Combine all the ingredients in a shaker.

- Pour the mixture into a glass over a crushed ice.

## CHEF'S NOTE

*Pious leader of the religious fanatics The Sparrows, The High Sparrow used the faith militant to manipulate the population of King's Landing for his own political ambitions. Along the way he punished anyone who took any pleasure from life, urging all to confess their sins. This delicious cocktail would certainly fall fowl of The High Sparrows rules against pleasure.*

# The White Walker

---

## Serves 1

## INGREDIENTS

- 120ml/4oz of double cream
- 60ml/2oz of vodka
- 60ml/2oz of blue curacao

## METHOD

- Fill a glass with ice and pour in the cream.

- Pour in the vodka.

- Mix and finish by pouring in the Blue Curacao.

---

### ◄ CHEF'S NOTE ►

*The White Walkers are a fearsome race of ice creatures, fear of which seems to have war for the iron throne on the backburner for now. Tall and white with glowing blue eyes, the cream and curacao in this drink echoes the appearance of Westeros' greatest threat.*

# The Three Eyed Raven

### Serves 1

## INGREDIENTS

- 25ml/1floz apple schnapps
- 25ml/1floz vodka
- 25ml/1floz apple juice
- Slice of apple to garnish
- 2 handfuls of ice

## METHOD

- In a cocktail shaker full of ice, mix the apple schnapps, vodka and apple juice.

- Mix well.

- Pour into a martini glasses.

- Garnish with a slice of apple.

### ◄ CHEF'S NOTE ►

*Bran Stark may never be able to walk again but he can fly as the three-eyed raven, taking over an ancient role and gaining the ability to see the past, the present and the future. The immense magical ability is founded on knowledge, so what better way to honor him than with a drink made from the symbol of knowledge, an apple.*

# The Night's Watch

## Serves 6

### INGREDIENTS

- 1 can Guinness
- 1 bottle Champagne

### METHOD

- Lay out 6 champagne flutes.

- Half fill a Champagne flute with Guinness.

- Top with Champagne and serve immediately.

### ◄ CHEF'S NOTE ►

*Inspired by the thick black cloaks the Night's Watch wear as they guard The Wall, protecting the Seven Kingdoms from White Walkers, wildings and giants. The Watch is a band of brothers sworn together by an ancient oath and this is a 'manly' drink - black like the Watch's castle namesake, and with a bitter edge.*

# The Moon Door

## Serves 1

## INGREDIENTS

- 25ml/1floz gin
- 25ml/1floz apricot brandy
- 25ml/1floz cointreau or triple sec
- Dash of Galliano
- Dash of lemon Juice
- A few ice cubes
- 1 maraschino cherry for garnish

## METHOD

- Add all of the ingredients (except the cherry) to a mixing glass.

- Stir well.

- Strain into a chilled cocktail glass and garnish with a maraschino cherry.

## ◄ CHEF'S NOTE ►

*This version of the Moon River cocktail is a tribute to the ancestral home of House Arryn- the Eyrie. An impregnable fortress situated in the Mountains of the Moon, it contains the deadly Moon Door which opens to the sky with a 600ft drop to the valley below. The door has proved deadly to many - as may too many of these drinks with the quadruple hit of alcohol!*

# The Red Viper

## Serves 1

## INGREDIENTS

- 25ml/1floz sweet vermouth
- 75ml/3floz bourbon
- 1 dash Angostura bitters
- 1 maraschino cherry
- 1 twist orange peel to garnish
- Ice cubes

## METHOD

- Combine the vermouth, bourbon and bitters with 2 - 3 ice cubes in a mixing glass. Stir gently.

- Place the cherry in a chilled cocktail glass and strain the whiskey mixture over.

- Rub the cut edge of the orange peel over the rim of the glass and twist it over the drink to release the oils and drop it in.

### ◄ CHEF'S NOTE ►

*This red concoction is in memory of The Red Viper- Oberyn Martell, the hot-headed, passionate and forceful Dornish prince with a penchant for red clothing. His skills almost let him finish The Mountain, but his flair for the dramatic allowed him to be defeated at the last moment. Try not to think of his crushed skull if you want to keep it down.*

# The Unsullied

## Serves 1

## INGREDIENTS

- 75ml/3floz gin
- 25ml/1floz dry vermouth
- Optional garnish: 1 or 2 olives or a twist of lemon
- Ice cubes

## METHOD

- Fill a mixing glass with ice cubes.

- Combine the gin and vermouth and stir well.

- Strain into a chilled cocktail glass and garnish with olives or a lemon twist.

## CHEF'S NOTE

*In the glass this pure clear liquid may look unsullied, but like its namesake - the elite warrior army of eunuchs, who now serve Queen Daenerys - the drink is strong, cool, calm and collected. A classic.*

# Test your knowledge of Westeros and the Known World

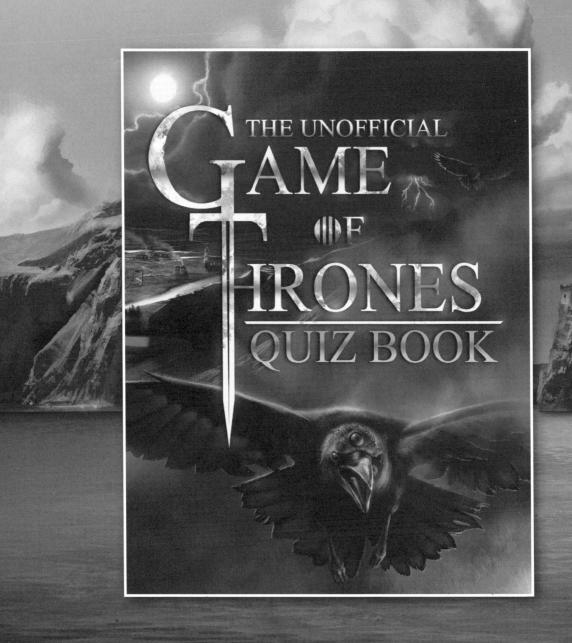

THE UNOFFICIAL

GAME OF THRONES

QUIZ BOOK